STO

ACPL ITEM
DISCARDED

10-23-72

Britain and the
Making of Europe

Also by Ian Davidson

The Gold War (with Gordon Weil)

Ian Davidson

Britain and the Making of Europe

St. Martin's Press . New York

AFFILIATED PUBLISHERS:
Macmillan & Company, Limited, London –
also at Bombay, Calcutta, Madras and
Melbourne – The Macmillan
Company of Canada, Limited, Toronto

St. Martin's Press   ·   New York

1717094

To Jenny

Preface

Brussels is a strange setting for the home of the new Europe. Its attractions are domestic and bourgeois; much of it is ugly to look at, but its solid middle class enjoys all the comforts of solid suburban living. It has an excellent ballet company, but it has few of the other attributes of an international capital city. Expatriate Parisians never cease to complain of boredom. It is not an exciting city.

Yet the institutions of the European Community are the centre of an almost permanent sense of excitement. Perhaps I exaggerate slightly; perhaps a better word is 'intensity'; perhaps this intensity is only apparent to those in close contact with the Community. Much of the time, of course, it is submerged in the humdrum round of routine activity, and over the course of time it has certainly been dulled by set-backs and disappointments. But it re-emerges with every important proposal put forward by the Commission and at every major negotiating session in the Council of Ministers; you can sense in many (if not all) of the participants and observers a degree of emotional commitment which goes beyond the question of national interests, or the nicely-calculated less or more.

'The European Community is the most revolutionary experiment in international government to have been made anywhere for over fifty years'; some such statement has been made so often that it no longer cuts any ice. But in the corridors of the Council of Ministers, at the moment of breakthrough in an important negotiation, there is an almost palpable sense of history in the making — especially if it is four o'clock in the morning and the air is stale with cigarette smoke and warm beer dregs.

It would be absurd to pretend, of course, that the Community exists on an undiluted diet of idealism. It doesn't, and on the whole enthusiasm for the idea of Europe is in inverse proportion to political responsibility, and to age. *Si vieillesse savait, si jeunesse pouvait,* to adapt an old proverb. The Commission is paid to think in European terms, and more often than not it does so; the civil servants from the national capitals are paid to negotiate on questions which affect their national interests, and more often than not they close their minds to all but the narrow subject at hand. Progress is made when the Ministers agree to over-ride short-term national interests. Yet all too often the Commission's proposals are cowardly or short-sighted; all too often the Ministers remain deadlocked — and it sometimes seems as if the only 'good Europeans' are the full-time journalists who stay up till the small hours waiting for an agreement.

I must also admit that I have found the Community most exciting when things were going badly. I first arrived in Brussels in the autumn of 1962, when the first British negotiations were entering their final phase, and the long-drawn-out arguments with the Six over deficiency payments were turgid and tedious. Above all, they bore no relation to the only important question, which was perpetually being asked but never answered: 'Will he let us in, or won't he?' It was only after we knew the answer to that question, in January 1963, that the Community suddenly became exciting: for the first time, the Six started confronting each other over the fundamental *political* question, and stopped nit-picking over East India kips or annual price reviews.

The crises which followed, in 1965 and 1968, were in many ways even more exciting, because the political confrontation between de Gaulle and the Five was even more naked and brutal. I would not wish to be thought to be commending the Community on the grounds of its dramatic interest; it is simply that the ideological struggle, which lasted throughout General de Gaulle's tenure of office, was most interesting and most illuminating when it was not muffled by subterfuge and evasion. That particular struggle is not likely to recur, and the curtain has gone down on the drama of Charles de Gaulle the Community-killer. The odds are now less heavily weighted against progress in the integration of Europe.

In the last resort, you can't persuade people of the attractions of the new Europe, any more than you can persuade them of the beauty of *Cosi fan tutte;* either they feel it or they don't. Those who feel in tune with Mr Podsnap will not feel at home with an enterprise which puts Britain on a level with other countries, however reasonably they disguise their prejudices. If I have tried to keep my own personal commitment to some extent in the background, I would like to think that the story by itself will convey, even at a distance, some sense of the drama of the events.

Contents

And they who write, because all write, have still
That excuse for writing, and for writing ill;
But hee is worst, who (beggarly) doth chaw
Others' wits' fruits, and in his ravenous maw
Rankly digested, doth those things outspue,
As his own things; and they are his own, 'tis true,
For if one eat my meat, though it be knowne
The meat was mine, th' excrement is his own.

John Donne.

1 · Whosoever in writing a modern history . . .

Whosoever in writing a modern history shall follow truth too near the heels, it may haply strike out his teeth.

WALTER RALEIGH, *History of the World*

I am aware that this may be a dangerous book, for it may well reinforce the prejudices of the opponents of the European Community. It does not offer a neat tabulation of what the Community consists of today, for any attempt to draw a tidy picture of an immensely complex situation would be at best unilluminating, at worst positively misleading. It does not put forward a crisp demonstration, in pounds or percentages, of the advantages of British membership, since no such demonstration is possible. Instead, it gives a concise account of the major themes in the Community's development over the past six years, in the belief that this is the essential key to any understanding of the present situation and of the future prospects.

The story is not a pretty one. What started as an idealistic venture to create a new kind of Europe, with the institutional machinery for dealing with the problems of the mid twentieth century, rapidly became embroiled in a resurgence of nationalism. For ten years Charles de Gaulle employed every device of violence and cunning to fight the Community, and in time his chauvinism became infectious. The actual achievements of the Community to date leave a good deal to be desired, and their nationalistic confrontations are a poor monument to the ideals of the founding fathers. Yet it must not be forgotten that the Community represents a revolutionary attempt to find entirely new solutions for the problems of the relations between the nations of Europe, and it is still in its infancy. The Athenian city-state is still admired today, despite the execution of Socrates, and only the most blinkered would dismiss the basic premises of socialism on the evidence of the performance of the British Labour Party.

In strictly economic terms, of course, the Common Market has been

1

highly successful: tariff barriers between the member states were removed more easily and more quickly than they had originally expected, their mutual trade expanded very rapidly, and they grew rich. For these reasons alone the Six all regard the Community as essential to their continued prosperity, and membership will give Britain a similar opportunity to participate in faster growth. But while the removal of the internal tariff barriers is the foundation stone of the Common Market, and the best guarantee of its survival, it is not by any means the whole building. The Six could as well — or almost as well — have stimulated their mutual trade if they had set up a simple free trade area, just like Britain and her partners in the European Free Trade Association, and left it at that. But the whole point of the Community is that it was intended to be a good deal more than a simple free trade area, and it was equipped with decision-making institutions which enable it to go very much farther. Its political roots lay in the desire of its founders to create a new order in Europe which would rule out for ever a recurrence of the conflicts which had devastated Europe in two world wars; and they believed that the liberalization of trade would lead to a process of economic interdependence, which would make such a new order not only possible, but necessary. The essential questions about the Community today are, how far will it go, how fast, and by what means?

In negotiating terms, the first decade of the Community's existence was dominated by three problems: the removal of industrial tariffs, the erection of a common agricultural policy, and the question of British membership, and in most of the bargains between the Six all three of them played a part. The Germans and the Dutch, as international traders, had a strong interest in the free movement of industrial goods. France and Italy, on the other hand, had little experience of international trade in manufactures, while a large proportion of their population was dependent on agriculture. The negotiations which led to the Rome Treaty appeared to offer a balance of advantage between agricultural and industrial interests, and the pattern was repeated many times in the years which followed the foundation of the Community. In practice, the removal of industrial tariffs proved both simple and painless, but the farm policy was another story. The Six, like virtually every other country in western Europe, had large but inefficient farming sectors which had to be protected, for social, political and strategic reasons, against competition from the industrialized farming industries of the New World and the Antipodes. The creation of a common farm policy could not therefore be achieved by the removal of internal trade barriers, but required a harmonization of the methods of protection, which varied widely from country to country and from product to product. In the event, the Six picked on the simplest method they could find, which was to reduce all their protective mechanisms to a basic system of price support, by means of levies on imports and public intervention-buying, and then to harmonize their six price levels so as to create a single agricultural market. Yet despite, or even in part because of, the simplicity of the system, the creation of the farm policy imposed considerable political strains on the Community as well as on some of the member states, particularly Germany, and left them with little energy to tackle other areas where common policies might be needed. Today the Community has an agricultural policy, with common support systems and common prices, covering the vast majority of agricultural products; it may not have very much to recommend it, but something of the sort was politically necessary, and it does exist.

It is fashionable to say that the Community's only achievements to date have been the removal of industrial tariffs and the establishment of the farm policy, but like many oversimplifications, it is not really true. The Community has an anti-cartel policy, the broad lines of a common trade policy towards the rest of the world, and a substantial trade-and-aid policy for helping the former colonies of the Six. It has also made considerable progress in creating a common market for jobs, as well as in the tedious but essential task of eliminating administrative barriers to trade between the member states. Nevertheless, it must be recognized that the Six have achieved rather less than might have been expected since 1958, and that their most important and dramatic achievement — the creation of the common agricultural policy — has not been particularly constructive or successful.

But if the record of the Community to date is rather dismal, the fault is at least partly that of successive British governments, who at first stood aside in the hope that it would come to nothing, then attempted to submerge it in the Maudling Free Trade Area negotiations, and only tried to join after it was clear that the Common Market was a going concern. The 1961—3 membership negotiations took up what energy the Six had left after their farm policy and tariff negotiations, and even after the French veto in January 1963 the shadow of the British application hung over the Community for the rest of the decade. Though membership in fact turned out to be unattainable so long as General de Gaulle was at the Elysée, it was nevertheless a question which occupied a good deal of the time of the Six. I would not suggest for a moment that Britain should not have tried to get in; only that when the application came it was too late, and that London's spoiling tactics in the 1950s gave plausible if unfair grounds for suspecting that the British were only trying to join the Community in order to destroy it from inside. After ten years of battering, the door is now open, and the enlarged Community will have the opportunity to turn its attention to more constructive questions. During his decade in power, General de Gaulle's policy towards the Common Market had three strands: to prevent the Community from becoming anything more than a loose association of sovereign states; to prevent the admission of Britain and other countries, which might weaken his position in Europe; and to impose at all costs a common farm policy which appeared to serve French interests. The first two strands led to perpetual and sterile battles with the Five, and the third to a farm policy which is misshapen and ineffective. This balance sheet does not mean that the Community method has failed; only that for the first ten years it was not tried.

If the Community's principal problem in the 1960s was the creation of the farm policy, its principal problem in the 1970s will be in the area of international monetary and economic policies. This must inevitably be so, for internal reasons. The removal of tariff and other trade barriers has been so successful that all the members of the Community are now heavily dependent on each other's economies. Each of them gets between forty and sixty per cent of its imports from its Common Market partners, and any shift in production, consumption or prices in one member state is almost immediately felt in the others; a boom in Germany, for example, is directly followed by an upsurge in exports from Italy. Indeed, it is no exaggeration to say that the Six have drifted into the early stages of an economic and monetary union – but without having done anything to make sure that this union of interdependence works smoothly. On the contrary, they have continued to act as though they were still masters of their own economies, and they have tried (on the whole ineffectively) to evade the consequences of having created the Common Market, just because they have not yet fully accepted the inevitability of acting together.

But the most striking demonstration of the need for the Six to forge common economic and monetary policies has come from outside, with the monetary crisis which erupted in the spring of 1971 and sent billions of dollars flooding into Frankfurt. In contrast with the Deutschmark crises of 1968 and 1969, which culminated in the revaluation of the Deutschmark in the autumn of 1969, this was a dollar crisis: the speculators were not selling their dollars in Frankfurt because they had any particular reason to believe that the Deutschmark was likely to be revalued again, but because they had lost confidence in the value of their dollars, and no longer wanted to hold them. For too long the United States had carried on the ruinous war in Vietnam, and the soaring American balance of payments deficit had reduced even the dollar to the status of a weak currency. The dollar was far and away the world's most important trading and reserve currency, but in the twenty-four years which had elapsed since the Second World War the United States had seen its position decline in relation to Europe, to Japan, and to China. Since the early 1960s, de Gaulle had attempted to throw off the overpowering influence of the United States; by the beginning of the 1970s it was clear that few European countries could accept American leadership without question.

In a general sense, the dollar crisis of 1971 underlined the fact that the interests of Europe are not inevitably identical with those of the United States, and cannot be adequately defended by European countries acting separately. In a monetary system dominated by the dollar, the European countries are the principal victims of the massive American balance of payments deficit, and so long as they act independently they are bound to act defensively. In the spring the Germans and the Dutch partially opted out of the system in one way, by refusing to accept dollars at a fixed price, and the French partially opted out of it in another, by refusing to accept short-term dollars. Neither action offered anything more than a temporary palliative for a problem which could only be resolved with a concerted European policy.

In this context, a European policy should mean a policy including Britain. During the spring of 1971 the U.K. was not unduly embarrassed by the inflow of dollars, since it had a large backlog of debts to repay to the International Monetary Fund, and the build-up of foreign exchange reserves in the Bank of England offered a cushion to soften the balance of payments impact of joining the Community. But the consequences of a prolonged dollar crisis would be just as serious for Britain as for any other European country, and in view of the historic precariousness of its balance of payments might well be more serious. At the time of writing, it is not certain how the United States will react to the crisis, but there is a powerful American lobby which would like to reduce the U.S. deficit by imposing protectionist measures against imports. The risks of such a transatlantic trade war would be less serious for Britain inside the Community.

The international trade and payments issue offers the sharpest arguments for closer European integration, but it is not the only example. The Americans may, for instance, decide for balance of payments reasons to reduce their troops in Europe; the European countries could only fill the gap effectively if they decided to act together. The Americans may decide to press for greater détente with the Soviet Union; the European countries can only make sure that an agreement is not reached at their expense if they act together. Unlike the U.S., Europe is heavily dependent on imports of oil; with a concerted energy policy, the European countries would be in a better position to control their industrial costs. In none of these instances is it necessary to assume that there is a long-term opposition between the broad interests of the United States and those of Europe. But it is clear that, in the short term, these interests are far from identical, and may well be in conflict.

So far the Six have largely failed to accept the need for common policies to advance and defend their common interests. But this does not mean that the need does not exist, or that it will not become increasingly pressing. The gothic absurdity of the common agricultural policy and the doctrinal wrangles over supranationality prove nothing about the nature or the potential of the Community. By the end of this decade Europe's farming population may well have shrunk so fast that agriculture will have ceased to be an interesting subject for discussion, and the departure of de Gaulle should make it possible to tackle the questions of majority voting, the role of the Commission and the powers of the European Parliament with something approaching common sense.

These issues provide the essential background to the present situation, the fund of (often disagreeable) common experiences which are bound to shape the attitudes of the Six to new problems. Ministers and governments may change, or may be unfamiliar with the past; but it is in the nature of permanent institutions to remember, and many of the civil servants in Brussels, whether in the Commission or in the national delegations, have been concerned with the Community for ten or even twenty years. The record of the 1960s does not define the Community in any conclusive way, and it certainly does not pre-empt its future development; there is no reason to suppose that any of the decisions taken by the Six to date, or indeed any of the 'terms' agreed between the Six and the U.K. are immutable. But no newcomer to the game can expect to participate effectively unless he has some knowledge of the way the earlier hands were played.

I have not attempted to draw up a profit-and-loss account of the impact of Community membership on Britain, because I do not believe the attempt could possibly be helpful. It is clear that the short-term effects, in terms of higher food prices and the contribution to the Community budget, will be negative, and it may be possible to quantify this negative item for the first year with a margin of error of, say, twenty-five per cent. By the fifth year the margin of error is so wide as to make any forecast quite useless. The cost of food and of the budget contribution will be much larger, but by that time the British economy will have had ample opportunity to take advantage of Common Market membership. Whether it will use its opportunity is another question: it is difficult enough to forecast the behaviour of the British economy six months ahead, and any attempt to make a forecast six years ahead, taking account of all the commercial and psychological changes involved in Community membership, must come down to a matter of guesswork. Personally, I can see no valid reason for supposing that the British economy and the British people are separated from their continental opposite numbers by differences so profound and so permanent that they cannot achieve some of the same success.

But suppose I'm wrong; suppose that British industry proves hopelessly ineffective in meeting the competition of its continental rivals, that the advantages of growth and exports fail to appear, and that in the late 1970s Britain is faced with a net balance of payments cost of several hundreds of millions of pounds and with no compensating advantages; what then? In that case, it is perfectly evident that new arrangements would be made to reduce the burden to bearable proportions. The Community can only survive if all its members consider that they are benefiting, and there is not the slightest reason to suppose that any British government would mindlessly carry out terms which turned out to be economically and politically damaging. If the Treasury had difficulty in finding the foreign exchange to pay the contribution to the Community budget, the other members of the Community would have to devise some way of making off-setting payments from the budget to Britain, or would have to make do with a smaller British contribution. The blood-curdling scenario, according to which Britain could be rapidly and mercilessly reduced to penury by the harsh rules of the faceless Eurocrats, has nothing whatever to do with real life. The Germans have made large contributions to the budget ever since the farm policy started. They haven't liked it, and they've tried to reduce their contributions, but they've been able to afford the payments because they have simultaneously been earning even larger surpluses on their balance of payments. Does anybody seriously imagine that they would have made these contributions if they had been in deficit? That is why the government refused to put any quantitative forecasts in its White Paper, *The United Kingdom and the European Communities,* published on 7 July 1971: the best possible outcome can only be guessed at, while the worst possible outcome would not be permitted to occur.

If there is a real danger it is that Britain will fail to perceive the opportunities offered by Community membership, and I do not just mean the opportunities for trade and investment. The entire political and economic balance of the Community will be altered by its enlargement, and every aspect of Community life will be open to review. It is true that the Six are sitting in entrenched positions on policies they devised to suit themselves, but it is also true that the new entrants will, simply by their arrival, upset established patterns and practices. English will be spoken in the corridors of the Commission, and for the first time the French will find it difficult to dominate Community negotiations. Dissatisfaction with the working methods of the Community institutions is now so widespread, that the U.K. should not find it difficult to press for reforms.

In broader terms, too, the U.K. will have considerable opportunities for doing something constructive in the Council of Ministers. During the 1960s the internal progress of the Community was slowed down to a walking pace by General de Gaulle and by the debate over Britain's application. The Community may have been somewhat damaged in the process, but both these particular brakes have been taken off, and the way is open for a new move forward. Progress does not take place spontaneously, however, especially after a period of near-stagnation; it can only take place if at least one government – and one may be enough – is pressing for it. There is certainly no lack of subjects demanding attention, starting with company law and taxation, investment incentives and regional policy, economic coordination and monetary policy, public purchasing policies and the problems of the European aircraft and computer industries. In short, the Community could well be entering on a new and more constructive phase in its development. Whether it does so will depend as much, if not more, on the attitude of the British government as on those of its new partners, on its readiness to send top-calibre civil servants both to the permanent British delegation and to the Commission, and on its willingness to try to make something useful out of the Community. Enlargement makes it possible not merely for the Community to acquire a new momentum, but also for the new members to have a decisive say in the direction of further progress.

This book does not pretend to be a complete account of the history of the Community, but it does set out to give the essence of the major developments of the past six years. The farm policy negotiations are described in some detail, especially from the fixing of common prices in the winter of 1964, since the problems of prices and financing are still central to many of the arguments between the member states. The constitutional crisis of 1965—6 is also covered in detail, because it is impossible to understand the Community without being aware of its institutional mechanisms in general, and of the aftermath of its most serious political crisis. But I have deliberately left out all minor issues, in order to keep the story as simple as possible, and there is no account of the protracted international tariff-cutting negotiations known as the Kennedy Round; despite the initial reluctance of the French, the Community contributed enormously to the successful outcome of the negotiations, but, like the internal removal of Common Market tariffs, it was an affair which was completed and today leaves little or no unfinished business to influence the future. I have given no account of the first British negotiations in 1961—3, partly because they have been so fully and admirably covered by Miriam Camps in her *Britain and the European Community 1955—1963;* for the 1970—71 negotiations I have confined myself to an analysis of the nature of the solutions which were finally found for the most important problems. Neither negotiation was intrinsically interesting or threw any significant light on the nature of the Community; the most important fact about the first was that it failed, and the most important fact about the second was that it succeeded. Within a very short time, no one will be interested in the 'terms' which were secured in Brussels and Luxembourg, for they will cease to be relevant. It will be much more interesting to see how the Community works, and whether it can be made to work effectively.

2 · And then there were Six

In the years immediately following the Second World War, the idea of European unity was like the idea of virtue: everyone was in favour of it, but few people agreed on how much of it was necessary. Winston Churchill, in his over-quoted speech in Zurich in 1946, said: 'We must build a kind of United States of Europe', and his phrase became the slogan of all those who were most committed to European unification; it was subsequently incorporated by Jean Monnet, the high priest of the European cult, in the title of his international political pressure group, the Action Committee for the United States of Europe. But in Churchill's view this United States was something which ought to be created by the continental European countries, but which was not necessary or appropriate for Britain; his view was shared, broadly speaking, by the whole generation of British political leaders who followed him. Unlike France, Germany, Italy, Holland and Belgium, Britain had not been conquered or occupied during the war. Confident in victory, in the Empire, and in the special relationship with the United States, the British saw no reason to throw in their lot on terms of equality with the continental Europeans in any scheme which seemed to require a sacrifice of national independence or an abandonment of any of the truly British ways of doing things.

By contrast, the suffering and killing of two world wars, and the folk-memory of countless continental wars going far back into history, had at last brought the other European countries to the point where they were ready to make the necessary effort of imagination and political will to find new and more effective ways of guaranteeing peace and ensuring prosperity. They knew they had to take part in the effort to create a new order.

But they also believed very strongly that a new European order would only make sense if it included the full participation of Britain; they were looking for new and daring ways of overcoming age-old hostilities, and it seemed to many (especially in France) that their only guarantee against failure would be the whole-hearted commitment of Britain as an equal partner. If the unification of Europe made only halting progress at first, it was largely because of the hesitation and reluctance of successive British governments. It was only fifteen years later that the United Kingdom started to recognize that it was, after all, a European country much like any other European country. But by that time the continentals had moved ahead on their own.

That is not to say that the British spurned all the widely diverse projects for European cooperation which were spawned in the first five years after the war; they didn't. But they tended to go for minimalist formulae, and did their best to ensure that ambitious plans were watered down in negotiation. It was not surprising that many of them fell by the wayside or proved sterile.

Broadly speaking, the various schemes can be fitted into three categories – political, military and economic. Of the three, the purely political schemes made the least progress, if only because politics embraces every other aspect of governmental activity. At one extreme, political unification implies the complete merger of the political institutions of two or more countries, and this was pretty much what the Churchill government proposed to the French government in the darkest days of the war when France was falling. At the other extreme, it means little or nothing. The only purely political institution set up in Europe so far is the Council of Europe, which was created by ten countries in 1949. It was given a Council of Ministers and a consultative Assembly – but no powers. It has performed a valuable function as a meeting place for European parliamentarians and as an interesting forum for political speeches, and it has done good work in the protection of human rights and on a whole series of technical issues; but it has remained essentially a talking-shop, and by the 1960s its general air of well-meaning amateurishness was beginning to look more than a little dated.

After the formation of the Common Market, the Six came back time and again to the idea of 'political union', though the phrase meant a great deal less than it seemed to imply. In 1961 they embarked on negotiations for a 'closer political union' to supplement the economic integration which they were undertaking under the Treaties of Paris and Rome (the Coal and Steel Community, the Common Market and Euratom), and the assumption was that the first step towards this 'union' would be a regular schedule of meetings between prime ministers and foreign ministers. But it very soon became clear that General de Gaulle was working on very different premises from his five partners; he saw the new proposals, not as a step towards political union at all, but as a way of bypassing, and thus weakening, the supranational implications of the treaties. The negotiations broke down in 1962. Nevertheless, the very phrase 'political union' continued to have the same effect on the Five as Pavlov's bell on his dog, and de Gaulle was able to play on their susceptibilities to good effect for a further five years. Gradually, however, their gullibility was eroded, and by the end of the 1960s even the connotations of the term 'political union' had shrunk, until it meant little more than 'periodic discussions for foreign policy by the six foreign ministers'. In this much more modest form, the idea of 'political union' became plausible after the retirement of General de Gaulle in 1969, and in 1970 meetings of foreign ministers began to be held, both between the Six and between them and the four countries applying for membership of the Community.

The military and economic forms of European unification were completely overshadowed, in the immediate post-war period, by the dominant position of the United States. Britain, France, Belgium, Holland and Luxembourg signed a defensive alliance in the spring of 1948 in the Brussels Treaty, with the additional aim of promoting economic and social cooperation as well. But in practice the economic and social provisions remained a dead letter, and the military aspects of the alliance paled into insignificance beside the North Atlantic Treaty Organization set up a year later, and its guarantees of American participation in the defence of western Europe against any attack from the East.

In 1950 Churchill proposed, and carried, at the Strasbourg Congress of the European Movement a motion calling for the creation of a European Army, and in the same year Jean Monnet was instrumental in promoting a more fundamental scheme for the establishment of a European Defence Community; negotiations started in earnest in 1951. But after the Conservative Party returned to power that year, and despite all Churchill's earlier inspiration, Anthony Eden made it clear that the U.K. would not join the proposed E.D.C. as a fully fledged member. By the spring of 1952 the Six were able to sign a draft E.D.C. Treaty, but only after they had forced a very reluctant British government to agree to enter into a mutual assistance agreement with the Defence Community. In 1953 the terms of the E.D.C. Treaty were reopened by a new French government, largely because it was unhappy with Britain's very half-hearted commitment. In April 1954 a new E.D.C. agreement was signed, though the French government was still dissatisfied with Britain's refusal to join in, and when Pierre Mendès-

France came to power that summer he made a last desperate attempt to get the British to change their minds. He failed, and when the E.D.C. Treaty was put to the French National Assembly it was voted down by a combination of Gaullists and Communists. The E.D.C. was dead.

In order to save something from the wreckage, the Brussels Treaty was enlarged (under the so-called Paris Agreements of October 1954) to include Germany and Italy, and re-named the Western European Union, while Germany was admitted as a full member to Nato. From time to time during the 1960s the Western European Union appeared to offer the symbolic advantage of providing a ready-made forum for official meetings between Britain and the Six, but in military terms it remained wholly inoperative, largely because of the Gaullist policy of national independence and non-integration, which cut right across the policies of the other W.E.U. countries, and prevented the emergence of any effective joint European approach to defence questions.

When such a joint European approach did emerge, in the very late 1960s, it was inside Nato rather than through W.E.U. The United States was becoming increasingly embarrassed by its balance of payments deficit, and though only a part of this deficit was due to U.S. military spending in continental Europe, the Administration began warning the Europeans with increasing insistence that American troops would be withdrawn from Europe unless the Europeans made a bigger contribution to the burdens of Nato. Partly for this reason, but partly also because the Europeans were becoming slightly apprehensive at the way the United States was beginning to deal over their heads directly with the Soviet Union, they set up a 'caucus' of European defence ministers who met informally and privately for discussions over dinner now and again. Much of the driving force for these 'Euro-dinners' had come from Denis Healey, Defence Minister in the Labour government, who had become progressively converted to the idea of European integration. Familiarity led to action, and in the summer of 1970 ten European countries (Britain, the Common Market Five, Denmark, Norway, Greece and Turkey) announced agreement on a joint programme for stepping up their defence contribution to Nato by about $900 million over the next five years. President Nixon promptly announced that the U.S. would now not make a unilateral reduction in its military engagement in Europe after all.

Quite apart from purely financial considerations, the formation of the European caucus was warmly welcomed in Washington on political grounds. Despite periodic pressure from the protectionist lobby, the Administration had long supported the principle of European integration, primarily in the belief that it would offer America a partner in the responsibility of leading the free world. For the same reasons the United States continued to support the attempts of successive British governments to join the European Community; in economic terms this would involve a sacrifice of American interests, since it would increase Europe's relative discrimination against American exports, but this sacrifice was considered a small price to pay for the advantages of being able to deal with a united Europe which, in time, would be able to speak with one voice.

In the economic field, European integration started earlier and moved faster than in either the political or the military. For the first few years after the war, the most pressing problem was the physical reconstruction of their war-torn economies, and their major diplomatic activities centred on the allocation of Marshall aid from the United States. But very soon the governments of Europe — or at least some of them — were ready to move ahead on their own. Belgium, Holland and Luxembourg decided to pool forces in 'Benelux' in 1947, and two years later agreed to work towards complete economic union. In 1948 France and Italy agreed to set up a customs union, and in the following spring decided to follow the Benelux example in setting up an economic union. In practice, however, the Benelux union failed to progress very far, while the Franco-Italian project never got off the ground at all, and the effective foundations of the new European order were not laid until 9 May 1950.

That was the day Robert Schuman, the French Foreign Minister, announced his plan for the pooling of the coal and steel industries of France and Germany, in a community which would be open to all European countries. The novelty and the appeal of the Schuman Plan was its astute combination of narrow, practical and immediate tasks and far-reaching political aspirations. The immediate aim of the pooling of coal and steel was to set the seal on Franco-German friendship and ensure that they could never go to war with each other again. The long-term aim was to create a European federation, and as a start Schuman proposed that the participating governments should surrender power over coal and steel to an independent, supranational High Authority.

Before the month was out, Germany, Italy, Holland, Belgium and Luxembourg had all agreed to negotiate on the basis of the French declaration; the British government, by contrast, could not accept the Schuman Plan even as the starting point for discussions, and negotiations took place without them. Less than a year later the Paris

Treaty establishing the European Coal and Steel Community was signed by the Six, in which they declared they were 'resolved to substitute for historic rivalries a fusion of their essential interests; to establish, by creating an economic community, the foundation of a wider and deeper community among peoples long divided by bloody conflicts; and to lay the bases of institutions capable of giving direction to their future common destiny'.

Beside these lofty aspirations, the bulk of the Paris Treaty is humdrum, legalistic and technical, with enormously elaborate rules for ensuring free trade and fair competition between the coal and steel industries of the six member countries. In the event, it turned out that the Treaty's rules were too precise, too elaborate and too rigid, and that the attempt to transfer in one jump national powers to a supranational authority was somewhat premature, even in a field which was confined to no more than two industries. Nevertheless, for all its imperfections, the European Coal and Steel Community (E.C.S.C.) contained the essential ingredients which were subsequently incorporated in the Common Market and in Euratom: a practical programme for the gradual elimination of economic barriers between the member states, and a framework of independent institutions which could not merely supervise the carrying-out of the programme and ensure that it really did contribute to the joint interest of the member states, but also take decisions on new steps in the fullness of time. This recipe, for moderate and precise short-term obligations but unlimited long-term possibilities, for an institutional framework which points in the direction of federalism but allows the member states to move along the road at their own pace, and for a programme of action which is both practical and idealistic – this is the essence of the European Community, and the recipe was enlarged and refined six years later when the Six established the European Economic Community and the European Atomic Energy Community. In all three cases the immediate, practical objective was the creation of a large European market through the removal of national barriers on the movement of goods, people and services; but the broader aim of coordinating national policies and pooling national decisions by means of independent Community institutions was apparent on every page of the Treaties.

Why did the Six draft their Treaties with these supranational if long-term implications? In the first instance, they were looking for a permanent way out of their long history of continental war, and a political community appeared the best effective guarantee against another war involving Germany. Today the political argument would be slanted rather differently – only a united Europe, speaking with one voice, can expect to be able to defend the interests of its member nations – and while the need for Europe policies is most obvious in the case of international negotiations on questions of trade, aid and monetary affairs, it is already beginning to become obvious in the military sphere as well. But in any case, the founders of the Community knew that they could not stop short at a simple customs union. The removal of tariffs may stimulate trade, but it also exposes a whole series of other obstacles, such as safety standards, health regulations, labelling and packaging rules – not to mention excise duties, exchange controls, commercial restrictive practices and company taxation. The apparently simple objective of free trade and fair competition could not be achieved unless the member countries harmonized a good many of these non-tariff barriers, and harmonization demanded not merely decision-making institutions but also a central system of control and law-enforcement. Moreover, once these non-tariff barriers were harmonized, the economies of the member states would become increasingly dependent on each other, and they would find it necessary to coordinate their fiscal, budgetary and monetary policies. From that moment they would be within a short step of a fully fledged federation. (General de Gaulle consistently repudiated the long-term aim of a federation, and would only admit that, in some very distant future, the Community might turn into a confederation. By this he meant to suggest that the emphasis would for ever remain on the voluntary participation of sovereign national states, rather than on the central decision-making bodies, but the distinction is more apparent than real. Switzerland has long prided itself on being a confederation, but in the summer of 1971 even the Swiss came to the conclusion that it was time they gave the government adequate powers to manage the economy, like any other state.)

Nevertheless, it was this supranational implication which stuck in the gullet of successive British governments, whether Labour or Conservative, during the 1950s. Before the war Ernest Bevin had advocated closer European unity, but he refused to take part in the European Coal and Steel Community. Three years later, when it was clear that the E.C.S.C. was a functioning reality, the (Conservative) government asked for, and got, an association agreement with the new Community which offered some commercial advantages but imposed no supranational trappings. In 1955, after the Six had decided to broaden the scope of their economic cooperation beyond the coal and steel sectors, they invited the British to take part in the detailed negotiations. A

16

Mr R.F. Bretherton was dispatched from London to sit in on the work of the Spaak Committee in Brussels, but he made it absolutely clear that, while he was more than a simple observer, he was certainly not a fully participating delegate, and by the end of the year he was withdrawn to London, while the Six continued hammering out the shape of the new Communities by themselves. By the summer of 1956, when they had started drafting the Treaties, the British government began pressing for the creation of a loose European free-trade area, which would supersede the new Communities and contain none of their supranational elements.

But by then it was too late. The two new Treaties were signed by the Six in Rome on 25 March 1957, and they came into operation at the beginning of the following year. At Britain's insistence they also took part in negotiations on the creation of a wider European free trade area, of which the Community would have been a part, starting in the spring of 1957, and dragging on for eighteen months. In the end they were brought to an abrupt halt by General de Gaulle shortly after his return to power; but it is possible that they would have broken down in any case, so great were the divergences of view between Britain and the Six over the nature and future of Europe.

If Britain was unfortunate in being ruled by men who believed that they were set apart by history and by destiny from other Europeans, the Six were remarkably fortunate in being led by men with a European vision: Bech in Luxembourg, Beyen and Luns in Holland, Spaak in Belgium, Adenauer in Germany, Alcide de Gasperi in Italy, Schuman and Monnet in France. They were doubly fortunate that all these men remained at the helm long enough to conclude the Rome Treaties; had General de Gaulle come to power a year earlier, they would never have been ratified and the Community would never have been built.

As it was, public opinion in most of the six member states was deeply divided about the new Communities, on practical rather than doctrinal grounds, during the negotiation of the Treaties. The small countries were afraid that their industries would be swamped by the power of the Ruhr and that their autonomy would be threatened by the political weight of their big partners; for that reason they insisted on institutional rules which would provide guarantees for the protection of their interests. The French were even more frightened of German industry; for that reason, and because they were very skilful negotiators, they insisted that the new Community must contain a farm policy which would give compensating advantages to French agriculture, and must also take over some financial responsibility for

French colonies in Africa. These early fears started evaporating almost immediately, and within a relatively short time they had largely disappeared. The removal of industrial tariffs proved to be so painless that the Six were able to complete the process eighteen months ahead of schedule. French industry did not merely survive against German competition, it flourished and turned France within a matter of years into a major exporting country. Ludwig Erhard's 'German Miracle' became a byword for economic growth and prosperity, but it was soon overshadowed by the much faster growth of the Italian economy, and Italians who had emigrated to the four corners of the earth in search of jobs soon began flooding back to Milan and Turin. Belgium was remarkably successful in overcoming the handicap of an old-fashioned industrial structure based on coal, steel, textiles and glass, and Holland was transformed from a country of traders and tulip-growers into a country of industrialists.

Just how much of the economic prosperity of the Six is directly due to the creation of the Common Market is disputed by academic economists. What is beyond dispute is that their economies have grown very fast, that their governments have accomplished most of the short-term objectives specifically laid down in the Treaties, and that most Europeans ascribe their prosperity to the achievements of the Common Market. As far as the man in the street is concerned, the Common Market is a success.

Most of the rest of this book takes the success story of the Community for granted, since it is already past history. It concentrates instead on the prolonged conflict between General de Gaulle and the Five, since this conflict was concerned with the future of Europe. It was a conflict which remained inconclusive, because the future can never be pre-empted.

3 · For forms of government . . .

For forms of government let fools contest;
Whate'er is best administered is best.

ALEXANDER POPE, *An Essay on Man*

Perhaps the most important single fact about the European Community is that it is open-ended. The Rome Treaty which founded it lays down a number of precise obligations, such as the establishment of a customs union, a common agricultural policy, freedom of labour, a common commercial policy towards the outside world and a competition policy internally, as well as a time-table for achieving these objectives. But unlike the articles of association of many companies, the Treaty puts no limits on the future development of the Community. It was designed, as the preamble says, 'to establish the foundations of an ever closer union among the European peoples', and at no point does it say or suggest anything which could legally put limits on the closeness of this union.

This open-endedness explains the ideological battles between the member states which bedevilled its early years, just as it also underlines the immense importance of the Community institutions. There is no doubt that many of the founders of the Community hoped, and believed, that it would in time develop on unmistakably federal lines, and that the economic links established in the first instance by free trade would eventually form the foundation for political union. But if any attempt had been made to write this into the Treaty as a fixed obligation, there is equally little doubt that the Treaty would never have been signed at all. The only feasible course was to start with the most practical problems, like the removal of industrial tariffs on trade between the Six, and let time show how far and how fast they would go — in the belief that they would go right to the end.

If the anti-federalists like Charles de Gaulle understood the logic of this scenario, they did not welcome it. De Gaulle believed, with passion and determination, in the virtues of the national state, and did everything in his power to ensure that Europe would remain a 'Europe des états', in which the member states would cooperate where it suited them, but only where it suited them, but would remain independent in all the most important policy areas, such as that of war and peace. It may be remarked in passing that de Gaulle was not motivated simply by conservation: his ambitions for France had a hard streak of crude nationalism, and he believed that France's influence would be greater in Europe and in the world at large if he could prevent any strengthening of the Community's institutions in Brussels.

This dichotomy between the federalists and the nationalists has coloured all the major policy disputes in the European Community. Even where the particular question at issue has appeared to be of little importance, it has been regarded by both sides as setting a precedent for the future. At the time of the first British membership negotiations in 1961−3, for example, the French government tried to prevent the Commission from being present in the conference chamber. The Treaty quite explicitly says that only the member states can decide on the admission of new members, and that they must be unanimous; there was, therefore, no legal possibility for the Commission to dictate the outcome of the negotiations. But the French were anxious to prevent any precedent which might seem to strengthen the authority or the influence of the Commission. Their fears were to some extent justified: in the Community's internal policy-making − on tariff-cutting for example − the Commission was allocated a central role by virtue of the Treaty, both for proposing new policies and for finding compromises between the Six. It was not unreasonable for the French to fear that the Commission would succeed in extending its authority into areas not specified by the Rome Treaty, and every battle fought between the Six has therefore always had two sides − the substantive and the symbolic.

At this point it is necessary to explain in rather more detail how the Community's institutions actually work. Basically, there are four major institutions: the Council of Ministers, the Commission, the European Parliament (or, as the French long insisted on calling it, since they had little desire to see it ever become a real Parliament, 'the Consultative Assembly'), and the Court of Justice. There are a number of peripheral or subsidiary bodies, like the Economic and Social Council (a consultative group representing business, labour and consumers), the European Investment Bank, the Monetary Committee, the Central Bank Committee, and the agricultural Management Committees; but they are on the fringe of the main decision-making processes.

The Court of Justice is the ultimate guardian of Community law, and can (and does) pass judgement on cases involving private individuals, companies and even governments. Its existence is an important guarantee of the legality of the Community process, and its power to over-ride national law in appropriate circumstances is a significant precedent for potential federalism. But it does not normally come into the picture until the other Community institutions have decided what the law shall be.

The Parliament has its seat in Luxembourg and holds its public sessions at the Council of Europe building in Strasbourg; it consists of delegations from the six national parliaments, and its duty is to debate and discuss proposals for Community legislation. It does not, however, have any legislative power, either to enact policies of its own choosing or to veto policies decided by the Council of Ministers. It has a right to be consulted on all Community legislation, but its expressions of opinion have no binding force. One reason for this situation is that the member states, and especially France, had no intention of handing over any power to the Parliament. It also happens that the Parliament is not really representative, even at one remove; for many years, it did not include any Communists, even though they were present in force in the French and Italian Parliaments, and for several years, indeed, the Italian delegation included politicians who had ceased to be members of their own Parliament back home.

Since the early 1960s the European Parliament has been urging the member states to make changes which would open the door to direct elections to the assembly in Strasbourg. But this request, which would obviously strengthen its authority and transform it from a talking-shop into a real Parliament, has so far fallen on deaf ears. The Dutch have always been the most vocal advocates of a more democratic Community; but it was not until 1970, when the Six decided to give the Community its own inalienable budgetary resources, that the Dutch government secured even a small increase in the Parliament's influence on policy, and even that small increase would not come into effect until 1975.

The Parliament does have one power: it can dismiss the members of the Commission en bloc. In practice this power is too wholesale ever to be used, and in any case the Parliament's main quarrels in the past have been with the Council of Ministers, but rarely with the Commission, which has tended to support its repeated demand for a bigger say in the decision-making process. In short, the Strasbourg Assembly remains a talking-shop just like the Council of Europe, with which it shares the amphitheatre and committee rooms in the Maison de l'Europe.

But there is one difference between these two debating groups which has struck anyone who has ever sat through their sessions: the debates in the Council of Europe are a great deal more interesting and lively than those of the European Parliament. One mundane but valid explanation is that the Council of Europe does very much less in the way of policy-making than the European Community. The European Parliament may have no power and precious little influence, but it is called upon to debate and express opinions upon the nuts and bolts of policies proposed by the Commission or adopted by the Council of Ministers; and though these policies have a direct effect on some aspect of the economic life of the six member states, they are often highly technical. The Council of Europe spends just about as much time on debates as the European Parliament, but since, for better or worse, it has none of the Parliament's technical chores, it can and does devote its talking sessions to the great political questions of the day – such as East–West relations, disarmament, the liberalization of world trade and so on.

A second reason, which may appeal to the British, is that the membership of the Council of Europe, including as it does most of the democracies or quasi-democracies of Europe, is much wider than that of the European Parliament. In some respects the parliamentary traditions of the lower house in The Hague are as strong as those of Westminster, but the same cannot be said of the other Common Market countries, whose parliamentarians are only too prone to turgid speechifying. The antics of the House of Commons are to many people undignified, and on occasion absurd; but there is no doubt that the debates of the Council of Europe are carried on at a very much higher level than those of the European Parliament, or that this difference is to a significant degree attributable to the presence of the British M.P.s. Nevertheless, it should be added that for all their relative dreariness, the debates of the European Parliament are regularly watched from the public galleries by throngs of visiting parties of schoolchildren, intent on seeing the Community at work.

So much for the entertainment provided by the Common Market: now for the serious stuff – the Council of Ministers and the Commission. But before we can understand how these two institutions work today, we have to look back twenty years to the institutions of the first European Community, the European Coal and Steel Community, set up by the Treaty of Paris in 1951. Partly because this Community was narrowly concerned with only two industrial sectors and had no general aims of economic integration, partly because it was founded under the early impulse of quasi-federalist idealism, the Treaty conferred most of the decision-making power on the supranational secretariat, which was appropriately called the High Authority, while the Council of Ministers had, by and large, only a consultative role. But it gradually became clear that the Treaty was not really in tune with political or economic reality: its detailed rules were based on the assumption that Europe would be permanently short of both coal and steel (an assumption that rapidly proved false) while the federalist élan which accompanied its drafting was soon dissipated. European coal mines found it increasingly difficult to compete with imported forms of energy, the High Authority found the Treaty of Paris ill-adapted for dealing with the situation, and the member states became increasingly reluctant to allow the High Authority to use the powers it theoretically held under the Treaty.

So when the Six came to draft the Treaties of Rome, founding the European Community and the European Atomic Energy Community (Euratom), they tilted the balance of power in favour of the Council of Ministers, and called the two supranational secretariats Commissions, rather than High Authorities. Nevertheless, the federalists — or rather, one should say more precisely, the small countries in the Benelux — salvaged something from the relative failure of the institutional arrangements of the E.C.S.C., and secured for the Commissions a key role at the centre of the decision-making process, even if they did not have very much independent power. (From now on, I shall talk about the Commission, rather than the Commissions; partly for the sake of simplicity, partly because, since 1967, the High Authority and the two Commissions have been rolled into one single body, called the Commission, which carries out the relevant functions for all three treaties.)

The Commission's role is to propose policies to the Council of Ministers, which then takes decisions. But since in most of the areas laid down by the Treaties the Council can only take decisions on the basis of proposals put forward by the Commission, it is clear that the Commission has a very potent part to play. The Commission's position was due to become in time even more powerful, as the Council of Ministers gradually moved from unanimity to the general principle of majority voting, a trend which was scheduled to start in earnest in 1966; for if no individual member state was able to block a Commission proposal by a national veto, then Commission proposals stood a much greater chance of being adopted.

In the first few years of the Community, this theoretical pattern was very largely carried out in practice. The objectives laid down in the Treaty for these early years were relatively precise, both in content and timing, and there was not an enormous amount of room either for the Commission to make unexpected proposals or for the Council of Ministers to kick up a fuss. Perhaps partly for this reason, these early years were in any case marked by what subsequently came to be known, nostalgically, as 'the Community spirit': a readiness by every state to take for granted its partners' good faith, and to accept decisions which went against its immediate national interest, in the confident belief that on some future issue it would in turn receive generous treatment.

This 'Community spirit' was doomed from the moment when Charles de Gaulle came to power in France, barely six months after the Common Market started operating. He did not like the Rome Treaty, he did not share the ideals of federalists like Jean Monnet and Paul-Henri Spaak, and if he tolerated the institutional rules of the Community it was only in order to maximize French economic advantages and French political influence. Since he was also the toughest, the most independent and the most autocratic statesman on the continent, master in his own country and ruthless in his dealings with others, the federalists were gradually forced to come to terms with the fact that their early hopes might have to be postponed. By 1963, when he vetoed Britain's membership negotiations after they had been in progress for fifteen months, it was clear that he was a man who was determined to extract concessions, but would give none himself, and the Community spirit was dead. During 1965, when he boycotted the Community for seven months in an attempt to break the mainsprings of the Treaty, it looked as though the Community itself was in mortal danger. In fact it survived; but the blows it suffered at the hands of de Gaulle have left permanent scars, and the hallmark of a typical Brussels negotiation today is not the Community spirit but the package deal which gives something to everyone on a national basis.

The deepest wounds inflicted by de Gaulle have been those on the Commission. It may not have been given much supranational *power* under the Treaty − indeed, its only power by and large is to carry out the policies decided by the Council of Ministers or see that they are carried out by others. But it *was* conceived as an independent body, whose governing body (i.e. the President and eight other Members) is specifically forbidden by the Treaty to take instructions from the member governments. In fact each country has an agreed representation on the Commission (two each for the big countries and one each for the small), and it is only natural that the two German Commissioners, for example, will be more closely in touch with affairs in Germany than their colleagues. But in the early years, under the somewhat legalistic Presidency of Professor Walter Hallstein, the Commissioners remained pretty well above any suspicion of wishing to foster their national interests, and the proposals they put forward to the Council were generally conceived on Community lines.

The 1965 crisis marked a turning point for the Commission in this respect. The French government, outraged at a Commission proposal which would have accelerated enormously the progress of the Community towards federalism, refused to take any part in Brussels policy-making for seven months, demanded major changes in the Treaty (including a down-grading of the Commission and the abolition of majority voting in the Council of Ministers), and appeared quite seriously to be threatening to take France out of the Community altogether if it did not receive satisfaction. In the event, and somewhat to everyone's surprise, the Five stood up to the French, and in January 1966 the hatchet was at least half buried. But the episode was a nightmare for the Commission; it realized too late that it had seriously misjudged the likely consequences of its proposal, it spent seven months in constant fear that its independence might be permanently curtailed, and to this day it has never recovered its former confidence.

This became deplorably clear in 1967, over the Labour government's application for membership negotiations. Under the terms of the Treaty, an application for membership can only be decided by the member states after the Commission has given its opinion, and in the course of the long-drawn-out battle between France and the Five it was agreed that the Commission should give its opinion. In their debates on the drafts of this opinion the Commissioners were divided along national lines, with those from the Five taking a pro-British line, and those from France taking an anti-British line. In the end, it proved impossible for the two French Commissioners to sustain the French government's argument that negotiations should not be opened, and the Opinion duly concluded by recommending the opening of negotiations. But the section dealing with the economic and financial aspects of the British application was utterly damning, and it so happened that the Commission department for economic and financial affairs was the special responsibility of Professor Raymond Barre, a Frenchman, a known Gaullist, and an opponent of British membership. No one has ever suggested that Raymond Barre received instructions from the

French government; he did not need to, since the government's position was well known. But anyone who believes that the remarkable similarities between the economic section of the Commission's Opinion and the views of the French government were coincidental, will believe anything.

This was an extreme example of the Commission's surrender of its duty to be independent, but it was not an isolated case. After 1965 the Commission became timid in its anxiety not to make proposals which could antagonize the member states, and it spent a great deal more time than formerly in sounding out the governments before making official submissions to the Council of Ministers. In other circumstances this might have had advantages, if it had ensured more rapid progress towards European integration. In practice, however, the Community marked time during the remaining years of the decade, and the Commission merely forfeited, by its timidity, much of its previous moral authority. Walter Hallstein had some of the failings of an academic lawyer and civil servant, but he was a man of substance. His successor, Jean Rey, a former Belgian Economics Minister, was well-meaning but more light-weight, and under Franco-Maria Malfatti, a former Italian Minister of the Post Office, the Commission has ceased to be the spiritual leader of the Community. It still does very valuable work, and some of its members, like Dr Sicco Mansholt, the weather-beaten architect of the farm policy, still carry a good deal of political weight; but its role is much reduced.

The key weakness of the Commission is partly due to the jealous nationalism of the member states, especially France, who have done their best to maximize their own authority through the Council of Ministers; but it is also partly due to the way the Treaty was drafted. On paper, the Commission's position ought to be impregnable: in a great many areas the Council cannot take a decision except on the basis of a proposal from the Commission, and while the Commission can alter its own proposals at any time, the Council cannot alter a Commission proposal except by unanimous agreement. In the early years of the Community this procedure was generally followed, and it meant that the Commission was in a very strong position to influence the outcome of a negotiation. In the classic marathon sessions in the Council, a great deal depended on the Commission's astuteness in assessing each country's real sticking point (in contrast with its opening position) and on its skill in producing the necessary modifications to its original proposal at just the right moment (very often in the small hours of the morning) so as to ensure a compromise which satisfied both the member states and the interests of the Community at large.

But in reality, the Commission's position rested primarily on its effectiveness in action, and that in turn depended more on the underlying readiness of the Six to move together towards a more integrated Community than on the procedural rules written into the Rome Treaty. With every year that passed from the accession of General de Gaulle in 1958 until his withdrawal from public life in 1969, it became increasingly clear that there was, and could be, no consensus between the Six on the nature and future of Europe. Once the French had started resorting regularly to strong-arm tactics, to ultimatums, threats and boycotts, it became unrealistic to believe that the Commission's position could be strong enough to urge the Community forward. In theory, the Commission is the guardian of the Treaty and of the Community's rules and regulations; in practice, when the going got really rough, as it did in 1965, the Commission was powerless, and if any effective resistance was to be offered to the French assault, it had to come from a real political power-base – that is, from the other member states. In the first two years after de Gaulle's retirement, France abandoned its aggressively anti-Community stance and finally withdrew its veto on the admission of the United Kingdom. It is not inconceivable that the doctrinal battles of the 1960s will give way in the 1970s to an atmosphere of greater Community harmony, and in that case the Commission may well find that its position is somewhat enhanced. But experience has shown that its role is based less on the Treaty than on the consent of the member states.

In any case, the simple procedural rules laid down in the Rome Treaty no longer correspond fully, even on the most optimistic assumptions, with the realities of life in Brussels, if only because of the inexorable expansion of the amount of work that has to be got through. In 1970 the Commission enacted 2,448 regulations (mostly of an administrative character relating to the day-to-day management of the farm policy) and submitted to the Council of Ministers 390 proposals and 376 memoranda and reports on rather larger policy issues. The idea that the nine members of the Commission on the one hand, or the six foreign ministers in the Council on the other, could personally discuss all these bits of paper, is clearly only a polite fiction. The major arguments are fought out at the top in both cases, but the vast mass of the work has had to be delegated downwards to a proliferation of committees and sub-committees.

The process of delegation started at the Council of Ministers. Each of the six member states has a fully fledged embassy accredited to the

Community, called a Permanent Representation, headed by a Permanent Representative, which is in constant contact with the Commission and the other institutions, and prepares the dossiers for its ministers' attendances at the Council. Very shortly after the establishment of the Common Market, the six permanent representatives set up an unofficial Committee, known in the jargon as the Coreper *(comité des représentants permanents),* to hold preliminary negotiating skirmishes and sort out the technical issues from the hard political problems. Legally, decisions can only be taken by the Council of Ministers; but whenever the Coreper is able to reach an agreed decision, it is classified as an 'A' point on the Council's agenda, and all the ministers need do is affix their rubber stamp.

So important did the Coreper become in winnowing the paper-work, that in 1967 (when the three Commissions were rolled into one) it was given the status of an official Community institution. By this time, however, even the Coreper was unable to keep pace with the work-load, and it had spawned numerous sub-committees of its own, including a Committee of Deputy Permanent Representatives and several technical committees to handle particular areas of the Community's activities.

A parallel process of delegation went on at the Commission. At first the preparatory work for the Commissioners' weekly plenary meetings was handled in committee by their *chefs de cabinet* (corresponding roughly to a British minister's private secretary); then the Commissioners held meetings in twos and threes to look after particular areas; then more of the preparatory work had to be delegated to the deputy *chefs de cabinet.* Meanwhile, lower down the line, the staff of the Commission was involved in virtually all the committees and sub-committees of the Council.

In short, the simple principle of the Community's decision-making procedures – the Commission proposes and the Council disposes – is now quite inadequate to describe what has become a complex network of permanent seven-sided negotiations carried on continuously at many different levels. Because the Community is steadily grappling with new problems which tend to extend its range of responsibility, a great many of the decisions can only be taken at the political level of the Council of Ministers proper; and because the balancing of national interests usually leads to stubborn haggling between the ministers, the Commission does – or can – come into its own at marathon Council sessions. But the very fact that the Six are in permanent contact and discussion with each other in the Coreper and its sub-committees means that the Commission's exclusive right to control its proposals is significantly eroded. In a four-hour session, the ministers may be hard put to it to modify a Commission proposal off their own bat in such a way that they can reach unanimous agreement, especially if they do not fully understand all the ramifications of what is being proposed (as they frequently don't); in these circumstances the Commission can come to the fore as the honest broker. But in the days or weeks leading up to the Council session, the Coreper has had ample time to get to grips with the problem, and is in a good position to hammer out a compromise without the Commission's help.

Moreover, the Commission has a seventh rival – the Secretariat of the Council of Ministers. In theory, the secretariat only provides an administrative framework for the Council sessions: arranging the agenda, as well as all the necessary documentation, organizing secretaries and interpreters, keeping the minutes of the meetings, and so on. In practice the secretariat has long been jealous of the Commission's more glamorous role, and has done its best to secure a more important, if unofficial, place in the decision-making process.

In any case, the need for mediation between the Six in the Council of Ministers has become more acute since de Gaulle's frontal assault on the principle of majority voting. According to the Treaty, the Council was scheduled to move gradually from unanimity to weighted majority voting after the beginning of 1966. Despite its seven-month boycott from July 1965 to January 1966, the French government was not able to force the Five to acquiesce in a formal burial of the principle of majority voting, and the so-called Luxembourg Agreement of January 1966 was no more than an agreement to disagree. But the boycott created such a trauma in the Community that in practice few attempts were made during the next five years to reach decisions by majority vote, and never on any important issues. On the evidence of the record, therefore, the French government may be considered to have won an important victory against the federalists.

The verbal battles of doctrinaire extremists have little to do with real life, however. The federalist notion that the member states could be forced by the Treaty to bow to majority decisions before they were ready for it was obviously absurd, just as the Gaullist attempt to enshrine the opposite principle in a new legal document was super-fluous. It is perfectly evident that no infant Community is going to get very far, and may not survive very long, if some of its members try to ride roughshod over the vital national interests of other members, and there is absolutely no evidence that any of the Six would have wished to interpret the rules in this rigid way. For one thing, it would be far too dangerous: the Italian government for example, would never agree to join in a majority vote against France on an issue that could cause serious difficulties for the French government, for fear that next time round it might find itself in an equally embarrassing minority of one. For another, the point of writing the principle of majority voting into the Treaty was not to ensure that the Six would take majority votes on all possible occasions, but to provide an extra incentive for reaching unanimous agreement. If governments are aware that they *can* be outvoted on run-of-the-mill issues, they are much more liable to be cooperative and constructive in looking for compromises; if they know that they can never be outvoted, then the balance of advantage will go to the government which goes on saying 'No' longest. In other words, the battle which was fought out throughout the autumn of 1965, and came to a standstill the following January, had nothing whatever to do with vital national interests, but was merely concerned with the acute paranoia of a retired French general.

Curiously, a similar paranoia seems also to be present in Britain, and in its White Paper, *The United Kingdom and the European Communities,* the Conservative government chose to take up a meta-Gaullist position on the question of majority voting and national sovereignty. Unfortunately, it mis-stated the true situation: 'On a question where a government considers that vital national interests are involved, it is established that the decision should be unanimous.' No, it is not *established;* it is just the way things are bound to work in practice, and to represent real life as some kind of victory for Anglo-Gaullism is childish.

It hardly needs saying that the Community's present institutional arrangements are far from perfect; it is absurd, for example, taking only the most glaring instance of its inefficiency, that the major negotiations should be staged as tests of physical endurance, in which some of Europe's most important politicians and civil servants sit up until dawn before taking decisions. These marathons have become one of the familiar characteristics of the Community, but that does not make them admirable.

On the other hand, many of the stock criticisms of the Community institutions which are frequently voiced in England, and by Gaullists in France, are misplaced. It is nonsense, for example, to describe the Commission as a vast and powerful bureaucracy. Bureaucratic it may be, but its power is limited and its size is moderate; it has a staff of about 5,500, which is a few hundred more than the staff of Harrods, about 27,000 less than the white-collar staff employed in the

Department of Trade and Industry or the Department of Employment and Productivity, and about 95,000 less than the white-collar staff of the Ministry of Defence. Its bureaucratic vices are, to a large extent, inevitable in an institution whose task is perpetually being frustrated by the stubborn nationalism of the Six; which divides its time between the promotion of European integration and the preservation of its own position; and which, because of the depressing experience of the past few years, finds it difficult to recruit people of adequate calibre. If the member governments were ever to recover the confidence and mutual trust of the very early years of the Community and face with enthusiasm the task of building a new and integrated Europe, the institutional situation could be transformed. Many of the civil servants in the Commission today are disillusioned idealists, who joined the Community ten or even twenty years ago full of hope, who gave up promising careers in their national capitals, and who have stayed in Brussels for the money (which is good). If the Community were revitalized and started moving forward again, the Commission could expect to attract some of the best talent in Europe.

At the same time, more rapid progress would call for more streamlined institutional procedures, since even on the most optimistic hypothesis the present methods would quickly get bogged down. Federalists would like to see the Commission given greater political authority, with the nine or fourteen members being directly elected; by analogy, the Commission would thus come to play the role of a European Government, the Council of Ministers would act as a sort of senate, and the European Parliament (directly elected) would be a proper European Parliament. Anti-federalists, on the other hand, would like to strengthen the Council of Ministers, by keeping it in permanent session and by gradually detaching the Ministers for Europe from their national governments; reluctantly, they would no doubt eventually agree to a strengthening of the European Parliament. The second of these two courses seems on balance the more likely, because it would involve a more gradual transfer of power from the national capitals to the centre, and because governments are always reluctant to acquiesce in any diminution of their power. Whether, in an ideal world, this would be the better course to take, is another question entirely.

4 · The Farm Policy and the Crisis

France has two major assets in the framework of Europe, and two major liabilities. The assets are the professional skill of its negotiators and its enormous reserves of geographical space; the liabilities a large and inefficient farming sector and the persistent and irrational belief that its agriculture is, or could be made to be, an asset.

In the middle and late 1950s, when the Common Market Treaty was being negotiated, there was some excuse for the French government's obsession with agriculture. French industry was backward and under-developed, heavily protected against competition from imports, dependent for exports on perfume, wine and other luxury goods, and comfortably accustomed (by traditions going back to Louis XIV) to the pervasive controls of the French state. German industry, by contrast, was large, efficient and internationally competitive, and it was widely assumed that the removal of industrial tariffs in a European customs union would enable the German manufacturers to knock spots off their French competitors. Before agreeing to accept the risks of an industrial customs union, therefore, the French government demanded a whole series of quid pro quos – special privileges for its dependent territories in the Maghreb, joint Community responsibility for its colonies or former colonies in central Africa and, above all, a common agricultural policy to provide French farmers with the same free trade opportunities for agricultural exports inside the Community as the German industrialists would be getting for their manufactured goods.

At the time, it seemed a comprehensible position. But it was nevertheless based on a fundamental misconception of the appropriate economic strategy. In 1944 Henry J Morgenthau, the then Secretary of the U.S. treasury, had put forward a plan for neutralizing Germany, by dismembering its industry and turning it into a purely pastoral country. The Morgenthau Plan was discussed, and even temporarily agreed, by Roosevelt and Churchill, but was turned down on the grounds that this would be too harsh a punishment. It is only a slight exaggeration to say that, in the late 1950s, the French government was demanding a Morgenthau Plan for its own economy. Yet it should have been obvious even then that agriculture was never going to make France rich; if France had any economic future, it could only be as an industrial country, and not as the granary of Europe.

If it was not obvious then, it became very obvious indeed in the early 1960s. French industry did not merely survive the gradual removal of industrial tariffs, it prospered, and throughout the decade the French economy grew consistently faster than the German economy. General de Gaulle clearly recognized the central importance of developing an advanced industrial structure, since his diplomatic policy depended on the creation of an independent nuclear military force, and his administration spent countless millions on exploiting uranium, peaceful nuclear technology, the development of aircraft, rockets and rocket-firing submarines, atom and hydrogen bombs and miniaturized nuclear warheads. None of these things could have been achieved without a sophisticated industry. Yet his government continued to act, throughout his regime, as though France's only interest in the European Community lay in the promised common agricultural policy.

France *did* get some advantages from the farm policy. French agricultural surpluses were financed to an increasing extent by the Community Fund (that is, indirectly by food importers like Germany and Italy), and in the 1968—9 season the net French gain from the Fund rose to $288 million. This seems a large figure, but it needs to be put into perspective. Between 1958 (when General de Gaulle came to power) and 1968 (when he was nearly toppled from power by the May Revolution) France's gold and foreign exchange reserves rose by about $7,000 million, or by $700 million each year on average. The net foreign exchange receipts from the Farm Fund were therefore not required to finance imports of industrial goods or French overseas investment; if they served any purpose, it was only to add to General de Gaulle's accumulation of gold in the vaults of the Bank of France, as an instrument in his war against the dollar. There remain the savings on export subsidies for the farm surpluses, which did not need to come out of the French taxpayer's pocket, because they were coming increasingly out of the German taxpayer's pocket; but these budgetary savings were insignificant in comparison with the enormous and unproductive expenditure on the defence programme. It is all the more extraordinary that for fifteen years the French should have put their urbane and ruthless negotiating machine at the service of a peasant mentality. It was not the only extraordinary aspect of French behaviour during the 1960s.

Sensible or not, the Common Market's farm policy remained a central French objective, and they employed every available weapon and a good deal of their partners' good will to secure it; when legal arguments and legitimate bargaining ran out, General de Gaulle resorted to threats and ultimatums.

In the autumn of 1961, when a common agricultural policy was still nothing more than a general aim laid down in the Rome Treaty, the French had two levers to use against the Five: the British membership negotiations, which had opened on 10 October at the French Foreign Ministry in Paris, and the time-table laid down in the Rome Treaty. The French knew that any farm policy which suited French farming interests would conflict with those of a food importer like Britain, and they were determined to establish a French-oriented farm policy well before the British could get inside the Community. They therefore made it abundantly clear that no progress would be made in the British negotiations until a substantial step had been taken towards a common agricultural policy.

Secondly, the Rome Treaty laid down a time-table for the gradual elimination of internal barriers between the member states, and the first stage of this transitional period was scheduled to end on 31 December 1961. The move from the first stage to the second stage, which would involve further tariff cuts, could however only be taken after a unanimous vote by the Council of Ministers, and the French told the Five that they would not give their assent to the move until progress was made on agriculture. This was in fact France's last opportunity to slow down the time-table, since from the second stage onwards a unanimous decision was required for any further delay. The French had tolerated Bonn's foot-dragging during the months leading up to the German general elections in September, because German agriculture was even less efficient than French agriculture, and any common policy which appeared to benefit French farmers was likely to be unpopular with German farmers. But by the closing months of the year, when Konrad Adenauer had been returned to power, the French demanded action.

On 24 December, when the Council of Ministers adjourned for Christmas, the French were still dissatisfied with the progress made, and the ministers reconvened for another attempt on 29 December. On 31 December they were still not agreed, and by a novel fiction they decided to 'stop the clock' (i.e. pretend that the year had not ended) and meet again on 4 January. From then until 5 a.m. on Sunday morning, 14 January 1962, they carried on virtually uninterrupted negotiations; after 137 hours of talking, many late-night sessions, one all-night session, two heart attacks and one nervous collapse, they reached agreement on the basic elements of the farm policy and on the move from the first to the second stage of the transitional period.

Rolf Lahr, the State Secretary at the German Foreign Ministry, described the agricultural package as 'a new Treaty of Rome', and Konrad Adenauer said it was one of the most important events of European history. They were exaggerating, of course, and no doubt they felt they had to justify the fact that most of the concessions had been made by Germany to France. Yet whatever the balance of advantage in the final agreement, there was a widespread sense of euphoria in the Community over the creation of the first centrally-managed common policy. With the passage of the years, it gradually became clear that the policy they had constructed had serious inbuilt flaws, but even then none of the Six was willing to contemplate the abandonment of something that had absorbed so much political and emotional energy. **1717094**

The agricultural package which emerged from the marathon covered only a limited series of farm products — cereals, pork, poultry, eggs, fruit and vegetables, and wine — but the principles they incorporated became the basis for all subsequent extensions of the farm policy. Farmers were to get all their income from the market-place (i.e. from the consumer), and not from government subsidies; the minimum market prices must be fixed in the same way throughout the Community, and must be supported by the same mechanisms; trade in farm products must be unrestricted between the Six, and Community producers must be given a preferential advantage over imports from outside the Common Market.

The mechanism chosen to stabilize farm prices in the Community was the variable levy on imports. The free market price of wheat sold by the major exporting countries, like Canada, America and Australia, was always a lot lower than the Community price level, but it was liable to fluctuate up and down from week to week according to supply and demand. In order to maintain a fixed minimum price for imports, the Community needed to impose a variable levy, which could be adjusted to fill the gap between these fluctuating world prices and the fixed Common Market prices. Conversely, Community exports would get a variable export subsidy, to bring their price down to the world market level. It was possible, however, that for certain products or at certain times of year the Community would become self-sufficient; in that case there would be no need for imports, and the variable levy mechanism would cease to be an effective method of stabilizing internal prices. So the Six decided to supplement the variable levy system with a mechanism for support buying if prices fell more than a certain way below the fixed target.

In its simplest form, this was the system laid down in Regulation 19 for cereals. For other products, like pork, eggs and poultry (which depend heavily though not exclusively on feeding cereals), the arrangements were a somewhat more complicated extension of the rules for cereals, though the underlying principles of variable levies and internal support buying were the same.

Until this moment, the Six had had not merely different national farm policy mechanisms, but also different price levels, and for some products the gap between the highest price and the lowest price was as much as fifty per cent. By and large the French had the most efficient agriculture and their prices were lowest, while the Germans were least efficient and had the highest prices. It was widely assumed that in the long run the Six would have to harmonize their prices at a common level, if only because this would be the logical implication of the principle of free trade which they had already adopted for industrial goods. The French and the Dutch tried to get a firm commitment on the principle of price harmonization, but the Germans were adamant, and the Six made do with an agreement to freeze their prices at the current level. French wheat could be exported to Germany, but since German wheat prices were higher than those in France, there had to be a levy at the Franco-German frontier to bring French prices up to the German level, and a variable levy at that, to make sure that French exporters could not undercut their German competitors. Price harmonization and the elimination of these internal levies were left for another day.

In political terms the five regulations introducing these new marketing arrangements were overshadowed by the sixth — Regulation 25 — which set out the rules for financing the farm policy. The import levies would bring in revenue, while the export subsidies and internal support buying would require expenditure. No one could foresee just how much money would be involved either way, if only because the supply and demand situation inside the Community would depend wholly on the level of prices, and no decision had yet been taken on either the level or the timing of price harmonization, while the cost of export subsidies would depend on the equally unpredictable behaviour of world prices. But it was logical – or so the Commission argued – that the revenue from import levies should increasingly be employed to pay the cost of the export subsidies. Naturally the French agreed, and equally naturally the Germans disagreed, since this would mean that they as the major food importers of the Community, would thereby be the major contributors to the cost of the subsidies required to finance French exports. In the compromise which was finally hammered out, the Germans accepted the principle that in the long run the entire revenue from import levies would be handed over to the Community, and that all the costs of the farm policy (internal market support and export subsidies) would be borne by the Community, even though the ambiguity of the wording of the Regulation left room for considerable argument, both then and later. In the meantime, the Germans would only agree to a gradual application of this principle, for a limited period and with built-in safeguards.

As often happens in the Community, the precise arrangement was complicated. But it is perhaps worth spelling it out in some detail, because it provides the essential background for the battles which were fought in subsequent years, and especially for the crisis which blew up in 1965. The Six set up a European Agricultural Guidance and Guarantee Fund (Fonds Européen d'Orientation et de Garantie Agricole, or F.E.O.G.A.), which would progressively take over the costs otherwise borne by the member states: one sixth in the 1962–3 season, one third in the 1963–4 season, and one half in the 1964–5 season. On the income side, the F.E.O.G.A. would be financed in the first year by budgetary contributions from the member states, according to the percentage scale laid down in the Rome Treaty: 28 per cent each from France, Germany and Italy, 7.9 per cent each from Belgium and Holland, and 0.2 per cent from Luxembourg. In the second year (1963–4), 90 per cent of the costs of the F.E.O.G.A. would be met according to this scale, while the remaining 10 per cent would be covered by the member states in proportion to their net food imports. And in the third year (1964–5), 80 per cent of the costs of the Fund would be met according to the budgetary scale, with 20 per cent in proportion to net food imports. In other words, the German government had managed to put brakes on both sides of the farm fund balance sheet; there would be a slow increase in the size of the fund, and an equally slow increase in the relative contribution of the food-importing countries. They secured a three-year time limit on the new financing arrangement and, if that was not enough, they also got an agreement from their partners that the effective German contribution to the Fund should not rise above 31 per cent.

The euphoria of January 1962 did not last very long. Exactly one year later, General de Gaulle vetoed Britain's membership negotiations, and the Germans became even more reluctant to make further concessions to the French in the agriculture field, whether in extending the policy to cover other farm products like beef, butter and cheese, or in agreeing to any harmonization of prices. The price issue was particularly intractable, because the Six were quite unable to agree on any objective criteria for setting common levels. Common sense suggested that straightforward bargaining would lead to a common price roughly half way between French and German levels. But Konrad Adenauer's Christian Democrat government was extremely reluctant to accept any cut in domestic farm prices, since it was politically dependent on the votes of Germany's large farming population.

In an effort to find a way round their deadlock, the Six spent months trying to define the sort of price levels that would be required to provide an adequate income for economically viable Community family farms. But inevitably this prolonged exercise in semantic gymnastics failed to produce any agreed form of words, and it did nothing to make the political problems of creating common prices any easier. The Commission tried to alleviate the German government's problems, by proposing a gradual harmonization of prices, with a small reduction in the German level and a small increase in the French level; but in fact it only made things more difficult, since it would drag out over several years the political strain of selling a farm price reduction to the German peasants.

In the late autumn of 1963 the Commission changed tack entirely, and proposed that the Six should harmonize their cereal prices at one fell swoop, at a level more or less half way between the top and the bottom of the existing range, to come into effect the following year. The discussions between the Six got nowhere during the closing months of 1963, and in the spring the Commission revised its proposal to the extent of suggesting that the harmonized prices should come into effect in 1966, rather than in 1964. Again the Six were deadlocked, and in June, with the 1964 season almost upon them, they simply decided to prolong the existing price levels for a further year.

In the autumn of 1964, however, the French government started pressing very much harder for price harmonization than it had done in the spring. By threatening to take France out of the Common Market, it had forced the Five at a fifteen-day marathon session the previous Christmas, to agree to new marketing rules for beef, dairy products and rice. Now General de Gaulle started brandishing the same kind of ultimatum at the Five if they procrastinated any longer on common prices. After a French cabinet meeting in October, it was announced that 'France would cease to participate' in the Community if the agriculture policy were not 'organized as it had been agreed that it would be organized'. In fact there was no agreement that cereal prices should be harmonized at any particular date in the near future, but the French threat had its effect. On 1 December Ludwig Erhard, Adenauer's successor as German Chancellor, announced in the Bundestag his government's acceptance of the principle of price harmonization, provided it did not take place before the 1967–8 season. In another farm policy marathon in Brussels, which ran from 10–15 December, the Six adopted the price proposals put forward twelve months earlier by the Commission. To sweeten the pill for the Bonn government, they accepted the date of 1967, and they also agreed that farmers in the high-price countries (Germany, Italy and Luxembourg) should receive subsidies to compensate for their loss of income.

After so much sweat and argument, the agreement on price harmonization was greeted with almost as much elation as the first farm package deal three years earlier. Despite the distasteful aspects of the French government's strong-arm tactics, the member states had demonstrated their capacity for taking hard political decisions in the interest of a common Community policy, and there were many people who believed that the Six were now set irrevocably on the road to rapid economic integration.

For the Six had not merely fixed common cereal prices; they had fixed them in such a way that they would remain common, whatever happened to their national exchange rates. If they had merely fixed them in terms of national currencies at existing rates of exchange, and if subsequently the French franc were to be devalued, for example, French farm prices would no longer be at the same level as those in the other Common Market countries. In a freely competitive market, this would be accepted not merely as a reasonable consequence of devaluation, but as the main point of devaluing, since it would make French exports more competitive. The farming industries of the Six were not freely competitive, however, and the whole object of the common agricultural policy was to replace national protection with Community-wide rules to regulate and control the market for farm products. The object may have been premature and the methods foolish, but it was the only policy they had.

The Six needed, therefore, an objective standard of value for their common farm prices, and since it would have been invidious to pick on one of their national currencies, they chose what seemed to be the only stable standard of value – gold. For convenience's sake, they labelled their common prices in terms of a newly-created 'unit of account', equal to one American dollar's worth of gold at the official price of $35 an ounce.

Right from the start, it was recognized that this gold value standard would have serious implications. In normal circumstances it would have no practical effects: European farmers would continue to be paid in their national currencies, and so long as the Common Market currencies remained at their 1964 exchange rates, it did not matter whether people thought of the prices in francs, lire, guilder or units of account. Nor would it have any effect if all the six member states moved their currencies simultaneously in relation to gold and the dollar, in the same direction (up or down), and by the same amount; the Community would simply change the value of their 'unit of account' by the same amount, and domestic farm prices in the member states would remain unchanged.

In practice, of course, it was much more likely that changes in exchange rates would be confined to one or two countries in the Community, and in that case the link between gold and farm prices would really start to bite, and could create serious difficulties. If Germany were to increase the value of the Deutschmark in relation to gold and the dollar, it would be obliged to reduce the prices paid to its farmers in terms of Deutschmarks, in order to maintain equality with prices in France and Holland, and that would obviously be highly unpopular with the German farming population. If France were to reduce the value of the franc in relation to the dollar it would, according to the rules, be obliged to raise the prices paid in francs to its farmers. That would no doubt be very popular with the French farmers, but it would be correspondingly unpopular with the rest of the French population, and by intensifying inflationary pressures would work against the results which the devaluation had been intended to achieve in the first place.

It was widely assumed, therefore, that the gold-based system of common prices would make alterations in national exchange rates extremely difficult, if not actually impossible. According to Robert Marjolin, the French Vice-President of the Commission in charge of economic questions, the agreement on common cereal prices had transformed the whole issue of monetary union in the Community from a dream into a necessity. If the Six could not alter their exchange rates, except at some serious political or economic cost, they would find it essential to take steps to make sure that their exchange rates never needed to be devalued or revalued. This in turn would mean that they must coordinate their fiscal, budgetary and monetary policies, so as to keep their economies in line with one another.

Hence Marjolin's dictum, and though his optimism proved decidedly premature, it was widely shared and gave rise to a fresh burst of activity in the Community. In January 1965 the Commission proposed that the Six should accelerate the reduction of their internal tariffs on industrial goods (which were now down to only thirty per cent of their original level) so as to eliminate them entirely on 1 July 1967, and thus establish free trade for farm products and manufactures at the same time. In March the Six finally agreed on the merger of the institutions of the three Communities (the Common Market, Euratom and the Coal and Steel Community); in order to pacify the Luxembourgers, who would lose the High Authority of the E.C.S.C., they conceded that the Court of Justice, the European Investment Bank and the legal services of the Community should be located in Luxembourg, and that the Council of Ministers should hold its meetings in Luxembourg three months in the year. (*Je ne suis pas au pourboire,* commented the Luxembourg Foreign Minister stiffly at one point during the haggling, a remark which was correctly interpreted to mean 'the bribe isn't big enough.')

Even the French government showed a renewed interest in European integration: towards the end of March it called for the establishment of a new form of European company law, which would facilitate mergers between companies of different nationalities in the Community, and on 31 March de Gaulle announced at a cabinet meeting that he would be prepared to hold a Common Market summit meeting to discuss closer political union – providing France received satisfaction in the next round of farm policy negotiations. Such an overture from Paris seemed particularly auspicious; the previous discussions on political union had come to an acrimonious halt three years earlier, because the Benelux countries would not accept de Gaulle's attempt to subordinate the existing Community institutions to a new inter-governmental organization of Europe. No one imagined for a moment that de Gaulle's attitude towards the Community had changed in any fundamental way. If he had agreed to the merger of the institutions, it was primarily because this opened the door to a merger of the three underlying Treaties, and this would offer an opportunity to cut down the independence and the prerogatives of the institutions.

Nevertheless, the French government's apparent readiness to reopen the dialogue with its partners on closer political cooperation in Europe suggested that it might after all be starting to take a more charitable view of the Community in the light of the common farm price agreement, and might therefore be prepared to go beyond the immediate satisfaction of its national economic interests. It also seemed to suggest that the common farm price agreement had given France such a large economic stake in the continued functioning of the Community that General de Gaulle knew he could no longer plausibly threaten to break or leave it in the event of new disputes with the Five. A great many people started to believe, therefore, that the catchphrase regularly brought out at the blackest moment of every marathon negotiation session – 'We are condemned to succeed' – might now, in a rather broader sense, be true.

The Commission accordingly decided to take advantage of the momentum created by the common price agreement, by putting forward far-reaching proposals for the solution of the major outstanding problem of the farm policy – finance. As we have seen, the rules agreed under Regulation 25 in January 1962 expired in 1965, and the Council of Ministers had instructed the Commission (during the common price marathon of December 1964) to put forward new financing proposals to cover the period 1965–70, to be adopted by 30 June. After considerable heart-searching, in which the hesitations of Robert Marjolin were finally over-ridden by the arguments of Walter Hallstein and Sicco Mansholt, the Commission took its courage in both hands and put forward a three-tier package of proposals which would have carried the Community in one enormous leap on the road to federalism and economic union.

Though the legal under-pinning of the proposals was highly complex, their essential content was very simple. For the two years 1965 and 1966, the Commission simply recommended an extension of the gradual process started in 1962, with the Community budget taking responsibility for two thirds of the cost of the farm policy in 1965, and five sixths in 1966. From 1 July 1967, when common prices started coming into effect, the Community would pay for all the costs of the farm policy, and its expenditure would be covered by the entire proceeds of the farm import levies, together with an increasing proportion of the revenue from industrial customs duties.

From 1972 onwards all the levies and all the customs duties would belong to the Community as of right; if this income was not large enough to cover expenditure, the member states would make additional budgetary contributions according to a percentage scale, and if it was larger than the expenditure (as the Commission openly expected it would be), then the balance would be restored to the member states.

The third tier of the Commission's proposals followed logically from the second. The channelling of levies and duties direct into the coffers of the Community, instead of via the six national budgets, would take very large sums of money (estimated at around $2,300 million in 1972) out of the control of national parliaments. Since some form of democratic control over revenue and expenditure must be provided for, the Commission proposed that the European Parliament should be given substantially increased powers to influence, if not exactly decide, the allocation of the Community budget. The Council of Ministers would still be able to take any budgetary decisions it wished, but it would need to muster a larger majority to reject the opinion of the Parliament than to accept it. For good measure, the Commission added that, once the members of the European Parliament were elected by direct universal suffrage (an eventuality provided for by the Rome Treaty, but so far rigorously opposed by the French government), total control of the Community budget would have to be transferred to the Community institutions.

When Walter Hallstein outlined the substance of these proposals to the European Parliament on 23 March 1965, he was widely acclaimed by all except the Gaullist deputies. But it rapidly became clear that he had seriously misjudged the reception they were likely to get in Paris and, indeed, the whole stance of General de Gaulle towards European problems. Until the end of 1964, his battle-cry had been that he wanted to build a 'European Europe', sometimes adding the rider that it should be a Europe 'from the Atlantic to the Urals'. Precisely what he meant by such phrases was never explained, but they certainly seemed to imply a central interest in the organization of a certain sort of Europe. Some time during the spring of 1965, however, he changed tack, and the idea of European cooperation (on whatever basis) gave way to a new theme of 'national independence'. In March he had appeared to welcome the idea of a summit meeting to discuss political cooperation between the Six, but in April he abruptly turned down a German suggestion on precisely the same lines. In the same month he put a much tighter rein on French negotiators, in order to ensure that they would not agree to too much in Brussels, and in subsequent months he stepped up his war of nerves against Nato. Finally, he began flirting provocatively with the Soviet Union, especially on the occasion of a visit to Paris in April by Andrei Gromyko, when de Gaulle spoke of an 'agreement' with Moscow over Germany's eastern frontiers.

Hallstein could not have foreseen this shift in de Gaulle's tactics, but he must have known that his ambitious finance package would inevitably come up against stiff opposition from the French government. At the very first discussions between the Six, the French made it absolutely plain that they considered the Commission was meddling in matters that lay well outside its brief, that Hallenstein had behaved offensively in revealing his proposals to the Parliament before he had submitted them to the Council of Ministers, and that there was absolutely no need for the Community to go into the question of customs duties or parliamentary control. All that was required, according to the French, was a new financing arrangement running from mid-1965 until the end of the Common Market's transitional period on 31 December 1969.

What no one could have foreseen was that the Commission's proposals were to become the occasion – or rather, the pretext – for an open trial of strength between France and the rest of the Community. Obviously, the French government was not going to accept the federalist aspects of the proposals, equally obviously it would do its best to secure a more modest form of financing arrangement to cover the rest of the transitional period, and the bargaining could be expected to be just as tough as it had been in every other farm policy marathon. But there was no hint that this time the French government would regard the agreed deadline as sacrosanct and refuse to 'stop the clock' if a settlement was not achieved by midnight on 30 June, or that the Community might be facing its first really big crisis. On the contrary, the bilateral meetings which took place between Couve de Murville and Gerhard Schroeder under the Franco-German Treaty at the end of May, and between General de Gaulle and Ludwig Erhard on 11 and 12 June, were if anything rather more friendly than usual. And while, in the Council of Ministers, the French were firm, they were not menacing; they simply insisted that there was no need to discuss the second and third parts of the Commission proposals.

Unfortunately, by the time the Council really got down to hard talking in the middle of June, the Commission proposals had attracted a good deal of support, at least in principle, both from the other member governments and from a wide range of influential European bodies, including the Community's advisory Economic and Social Committee (representing labour, management and consumers), Jean Monnet's Action Committee for the United States of Europe (representing the leaders of all the major political parties and trade unions in the Common Market, apart from the Communists and the Gaullists) and, of course, the European Parliament. None of the Five would have been prepared to endorse the Commission proposals as they stood, but they accepted the Commission's argument that the proposals formed a logical whole and should be discussed as a package. They would probably have been prepared to agree to the underlying principles of the package, subject to changes in the details and the timing of their application.

Until mid-June the French position was logically weak, because they accepted the first step in the Commission's argument. For reasons of national self-interest, they supported the idea that all the food import levies should belong as of right to the Community from 1 July 1967, when farm prices would first be harmonized. They even seemed likely to agree that the Community's industrial customs union should be completed on the same date, and there were signs that they might conceivably accept the principle that, one day, in the distant future, industrial customs duties should belong to the Community as well, and that there should be some strengthening of the position of the European Parliament. But the vital question was the ownership of the food import levies: once the French agreed that they should belong to the Community, which would have its own source of income *(ressources propres),* they had no reasonable grounds for refusing to discuss the rest of the Commission package.

On 14—15 June, however, at a meeting of the Council of Ministers, Couve de Murville backed away from his opening position, and thus neatly severed the logical thread in the Commission proposals. Regulation 25 had laid down that the levies would belong to the Community in the 'single market period'. Until now the French had accepted the Commission's interpretation that the harmonization of farm prices would automatically establish the 'single market', and that the levies must therefore belong to the Community. Now Couve reverted to the traditional view that the single market stage would only come into effect in 1970, after the end of the Common Market's transitional period, and argued that the levies need not belong to the Community until then. What the Six must now do, he said, was decide how the farm policy should be financed from 1965—9, on the basis of national contributions. In other words, the French government was prepared to make a sacrifice of hard cash, in order to prevent the Community from having its own financial resources or the Parliament from having any increased influence.

The Council meeting ended without any agreement or, indeed, any noticeable progress. Yet even then, within a fortnight of the 30 June deadline, there was still no sign of a crisis. In a foreign affairs debate held the next day in the French National Assembly to ratify the merger of the Community institutions, the government took a predictably anti-federalist line. Couve de Murville said that no responsible government talked any longer of an 'illusory supranationality', and Georges Pompidou wound up the debate by saying: 'We do not believe that integration is the right road to European unity.' But in other respects their speeches seemed to indicate that the government was still looking for an agreement with its partners, not for a pretext to create a crisis. On the contrary, after Rolf Lahr and Olivier Wormser (the Economic Director at the Quai d'Orsay) had held a secret bilateral meeting in Paris five days later, it looked as though some sort of compromise might already be in sight.

The final negotiating session opened in Brussels on 28 June, and though their fundamental positions were as far apart as ever, the six foreign ministers appeared to be making some progress on points of detail, notably on the idea that the industrial customs union would come into effect on 1 July 1967 and, more tentatively, on the principle that the levies and duties might one day belong to the Community. But on the central issue of farm finance between mid-1965 and the end of 1969 there was deadlock. The French demanded a new farm financing regulation to cover this four and a half year period, to the complete exclusion of all other considerations. The Germans insisted that any agreement for such a long period (which would be a concession to French interests) must be linked to progress in other fields, notably the Community's common commercial policy and the harmonization of taxation; and they endorsed the Dutch demand that something must be done to increase the powers of parliament. The Italians, for once, took the toughest line of all; if France was not prepared to discuss the Commission's package, then they were not prepared to envisage anything more than a stop-gap arrangement, which would merely extend the existing financing rules without any essential change for one or at most two years.

The Six continued their argument for two days, and by lunchtime on 30 June it looked as though some sort of compromise might yet be within their grasp. If the Five agreed to postpone the 'single market period' until 1970, the French might be prepared to acquiesce in the principle that from that date the Community should have its own resources. Some undertakings would be given on tax harmonization and the common commercial policy, in return for an agreement that the farm fund would be fed by national contributions in the meantime, though the duration of an interim financial regulation was still very much in dispute.

But during the afternoon the atmosphere suddenly deteriorated. Couve de Murville reverted to his original demand that the Six must settle the financial regulation for the rest of the transitional period, and only the financial regulation; and they must settle it by midnight. The hardening of the French position drove the Dutch and the Italians into equally stubborn opposition, and as the evening wore on they were joined by the Germans. Whatever had been secretly agreed between Lahr and Wormser was clearly no longer in force. Couve de Murville attempted late in the evening to buy off the Italians by proposing a scale of payments which would have been very generous to Italy and expensive for France. But in every other respect he seemed determined to ensure a breakdown in the negotiations. He rejected an offer from the Commission to put forward new proposals, as well as suggestions from the Five that the Council should 'stop the clock' and resume its negotiations later. At two in the morning, he announced that agreement was impossible (even though the Five were all willing to go on talking), and, in his capacity as chairman of the Council, brought the meeting to a close. The 30 June deadline was now safely past; the French government could legally claim that its partners had not fulfilled their obligations; the Community was in a state of crisis.

5 · From the Crisis to the Second Veto

Just how serious the crisis was, nobody, including Couve de Murville, seemed to know. After the Council had broken up he gave the traditional chairman's press conference, and announced darkly: 'Each government must draw the consequences.' But when he was asked whether the Community was in danger, he said: 'I did not say that. We shall see.' He had carried out the General's instructions to precipitate a crisis, but evidently he had not yet been given the next page of the script, and did not know how the drama was supposed to proceed, let alone how the General wanted it to end.

The next day the French cabinet issued a long, self-justifying statement, which concluded: 'The government has decided, for its part, to draw the legal, economic and political consequences of the situation which has thus been created.' The Information Minister, Alain Peyrefitte, added that no new negotiations were planned in Brussels, and that everything was at a standstill. The following week Jean-Marc Boegner, France's Permanent Representative in Brussels, was recalled to Paris for an indefinite period, and though the French continued to attend routine Community meetings, they refused to take part in negotiations at any level on new policies. They asked for the cancellation of a meeting of the Council of Ministers, scheduled to discuss coal and steel questions on July, and announced that they would not attend a meeting of the six finance ministers on 19–20 July. The seriousness of the crisis was no longer in doubt.

In the belief that de Gaulle would be mollified by a satisfactory farm finance agreement, the Five and the Commission embarked on a hectic round of diplomatic consultations in an effort to patch up a compromise. Paul-Henri Spaak, the Belgian Foreign Minister, whose position had been closest to that of Couve de Murville on the fatal night, imagined for a brief moment that he might be able to cast himself in the role of peacemaker. He and his Dutch and Italian colleagues all had talks with the French in Paris on 12 July, on the sidelines of a Nato ministerial meeting, but got no response at all. The Five disregarded the French demand for the cancellation of the scheduled Council meeting, and held it as planned – but they were careful not to antagonize General de Gaulle by taking any decisions. On 22 July the Commission put forward new financing proposals, in which it went just about as far as it decently could to take account of the known views of the French government; they were discussed by the Five at a further Council meeting on 26–7 July, but again without taking any decisions. France had, of course, no right to boycott the Council, and it seemed quite possible, in strictly legal terms, that the Five could take valid decisions on their own. But none of them wanted to escalate the conflict until it was quite clear what was at stake; on the contrary, they seemed only too ready to turn and run at the first sound of gunfire – especially the Belgians and the Luxembourgers.

The gunfire soon became very much louder and very much clearer. Georges Pompidou gave a comparatively anodyne speech on French television at the end of July, in which he argued soothingly that 'there are solutions for everything' and maintained that France was the most ardent supporter of European cooperation. But he introduced a new and more sinister note when he said: 'We cannot leave to a Commission which has no political function the question of deciding the French standard of living and the future of our agriculture and industry.' No one had ever imagined that the Commission could do either of these things, of course, but his words gradually spread the idea that General de Gaulle had decided to use the farm finance crisis as a pretext for launching an attack against the institutions of the Community.

Just over a month later, on 9 September, these suspicions were more than confirmed when General de Gaulle gave his semi-annual press conference. He barely touched on the question of farm finance, which was for him only a peripheral issue. Instead he concentrated his fire on the 'mistakes or ambiguities' of the Community Treaties, on the excessive authority given to the Commission, and on the whole principle of majority voting, which was scheduled gradually to replace the principle of unanimity in the Council of Ministers, especially after the beginning of 1966. 'The crisis was,' he said, 'sooner or later inevitable.' No one had ever had any reason to doubt de Gaulle's hostility to the idea of supranationality, to the independent position of the Commission or to the principle of majority voting. But never before had the long-standing conflict between Gaullism and the Community been so clearly and so harshly stated. Moreover, he gave no sign of being in any hurry to settle this or any Community problem; France would be prepared to hold discussions with the other governments – if they asked for discussions; but in the meantime he predicted a delay of 'unforeseeable length', adding: 'No one can tell if, when or how the policy of our partners will be able to adapt itself to necessities.'

Couve de Murville went over much the same ground six weeks later in a long and detailed speech to the National Assembly. But in addition to enlarging on de Gaulle's criticisms of the Treaties, of the Commission and of the principle of majority voting, he demanded an 'overall revision' *(révision d'ensemble)* and insisted that there must be a political agreement between the Six before there could be any resumption of negotiations on technical problems like farm finance.

It may have been this final demand which stiffened the resistance of the Five and thus tipped the balance against General de Gaulle. Paul-Henri Spaak had been urging the holding of a special meeting of the six governments, outside the framework of the rules of the Community and without the participation of the Commission, in order to discuss the French grievances. But if the Five had hoped that General de Gaulle would be satisfied with some informal 'code of conduct' to govern the Commission and the Council, they now began to suspect, on the evidence of Couve's phrase *révision d'ensemble,* that the General would be satisfied with nothing less than an outright revision of the Community Treaties, and might possibly be aiming at the complete break-up of the Community. If this were so, there was no point in offering gratuitous concessions.

So when they met in the Council of Ministers on 25–6 October (without France, of course), they issued a long statement affirming the inviolability of the Community Treaties, and insisting that all Community problems must be resolved inside the Community framework. As far as farm finance was concerned, they announced that they had agreed, on the basis of the Commission's revised proposals, on the fundamental principles which should lead to an agreement between the Six, and they appealed to the French government to resume its place in the Council. Finally, they invited the French government to take part as soon as possible in a special meeting of the Council of Ministers, without the participation of the Commission but under the rules of the Rome Treaty, to discuss the general problems raised by General de Gaulle and Couve de Murville. In short, while the Five were prepared to discuss the French objections, they made it clear that they were not prepared to compromise on any really fundamental issue. The French government let it be known that it would 'study and answer' the invitation of the Five – but not before the French presidential election on 5 December.

Inside France, however, the crisis was causing considerable alarm and was becoming one of the major issues in the presidential campaign. In a television broadcast in the middle of October Georges Pompidou said that the Common Market could not be a panacea for France. But instead of pacifying his audience, he only succeeded in adding to suspicions that de Gaulle was intent on taking France out of the Community. The farmers, in particular, became very agitated at this idea, and on 21 October the major farmers' union advised its members not to support General de Gaulle in the election. Jean Lecanuet, a centrist candidate in the election, was endorsed by Jean Monnet, and the government's European conduct came in for severe criticism from the employers, from the trades unions and from virtually all the non-Gaullist political parties.

When General de Gaulle failed to get the necessary absolute majority in the first round of voting on 5 December, and was forced therefore into a run-off two weeks later against the Socialist candidate, François Mitterrand, it was widely assumed that the Community crisis had played a major part in his set-back. In fact, it was probably less important than other, social and domestic, issues.

Nevertheless, de Gaulle adopted a much more conciliatory tone towards the Community in his campaign speeches between the two ballots, even if he continued to harp on his familiar objections to the 'myth' of supranationality. 'If we can overcome the trial of the Common Market – and I really hope we can – we must go back to what France proposed in 1961 and which did not succeed at first, that is to say the organization of an emergent political cooperation between the states of Western Europe.' In other words, de Gaulle was already dangling the bait of political union in Europe, as if the crisis had never occurred or would easily be solved.

More striking still, he also dangled the idea of admitting Britain to the Community. In the same television broadcast and in the very next sentence, he went on to say: '... and at that moment it is very probable that, a bit sooner or a bit later, England will come and join us, and it will be quite natural. Of course, that Europe will not be what is called supranational. It will be as it is. It will start by being a cooperation, perhaps afterwards, as a result of living together, it will become a confederation.' After his re-election on 19 December (by a small majority) he returned to the same theme: in his New Year address he expressed the hope that 'other neighbours' of France would join the Community on 'equitable and reasonable principles'. But if he thought that by flying this kite he could bring out the British as allies in his battle against the Five and the Community, he was mistaken: Michael Stewart, the Foreign Secretary, told the House of Commons on 20 December that the Labour government's conditions for Community membership were now easier to fulfil, but the government did not take any sides in the dispute. Nevertheless, it seems probable that the spectacle of the French President in electoral difficulties for the first time, combined with the friendly noises he was now making in London's direction (for whatever reason), played some part in encouraging Harold Wilson to take a serious interest in the question of British membership of the Community.

Shortly before Christmas 1965, the French government officially acknowledged the invitation of the Five (two months after it had been received), and it was agreed that the six foreign ministers would meet in Luxembourg on 17 and 18 January. There, for the first time, the French put forward a precise catalogue of their complaints and grievances, in a ten-point document which immediately became known as the 'decalogue'. The tone of the decalogue was harsh, contemptuous and arrogant, and its content was far-reaching. But it did not include any proposals which would require modifications of the Treaties: General de Gaulle had been forced to swallow the hard fact that on this point the Five were, for once, united, and could not be frightened.

As expected, the French wanted two basic changes in the operation of the Community: a severe restriction of the independence of the Commission, and a complete elimination of majority voting in the Council of Ministers. The decalogue demanded that the Commission should never put forward proposals to the Council until it had consulted the member states at the appropriate level, and it should never reveal its proposals to the public or the Parliament until it had officially submitted them to the Council. At the limit, this could have amounted to a demand for governmental vetoes on the work of the Commission, and at the very least would have undermined the Commission's ability to act as an independent motor for promoting policies which suited Community rather than national interests. There has always been room for criticizing, even on Community grounds, particular Commission proposals; but that does not mean that a national veto system would produce any better proposals.

Next the French criticized the Commission's drafting of Community legislation in ways which tended either to channel too much authority to the Commission, or to deprive the member states of too much freedom of manoeuvre. In their next indictment of the Commission —

the 'striped pants' accusation – the French criticized Professor Hallstein's habit of accepting the accreditation of foreign embassies with as much formality as if he were in reality the head of a government. And they went on to criticize the way the Commission ran the Community's information offices in London and Washington as though they were embassies. Finally, the French demanded stricter governmental control on the Commission's right to give information to the press and on the right of the Members of the Commission to make public speeches. In short, the French wanted to encroach on all the ways in which the Commission had been most effective, either in getting policies adopted by the Council of Ministers, or in a broader sense in spreading the gospel of Community integration to the people of Europe.

When it came to majority voting, however, there was no question of encroachment. Couve de Murville demanded that France should have the right of veto in the Council of Ministers whenever she wanted one, and whereas there seemed to be some room for negotiation over the numerous points affecting the Commission, on this issue he would contemplate no compromise. The Five would no doubt have been prepared to accept that no country would normally be voted down when its vital national interests were at stake, but they could not accept Couve's contention that only the country concerned had the right to judge what its vital national interests were.

If Couve had been forced to come to Luxembourg with a list of demands which was a good deal less far-reaching than the *révision d'ensemble* he had hinted at in the National Assembly, he had not counted on having to bargain over it. But he found that his intransigence was fully matched by the united stubbornness of the Five, and that in contrast with all previous experience in the Community it was the Germans, rather than the Dutch, who were leading the Five in opposition to General de Gaulle. This was the first time that the French had encountered unyielding resistance from the Germans; it was not to be, by any means, the last. And since Gerhard Schroeder, the Atlantic-minded German Foreign Minister, had taken the trouble to get his defence of the Rome Treaty endorsed in the Bundestag by all three German parties just before the Luxembourg meeting, Couve knew that he could expect no change in the German position, now or later.

The only result of this meeting was an agreement to meet again in Luxembourg, on 28–30 January, but it was clear that the French government had only two options: to walk out or to compromise. To sustain the boycott indefinitely was impossible, since the Five would soon start taking decisions, with or without France. To walk out would be not merely a self-inflicted wound, but also an open invitation to the Five to bring in the British – and there was no doubt that they had already started considering the possibility. In the intervening ten days it became apparent that General de Gaulle had decided to settle for the best available terms with the Five, and to put an end to the crisis as soon as possible.

As far as the Commission was concerned, the compromise reached at the second Luxembourg meeting was very much more moderate than the French government's original demands. Some limitations were imposed on the Commission's freedom to appeal for public support over the heads of the member governments, and it was formally requested to consult the governments before making proposals 'without this procedure affecting the right of initiative which the Commission derives from the Treaty'. But the new constraints were not very serious, and even the Commission argued that its effectiveness would not be materially affected. In fact, the Commission had never put forward proposals without at some point sounding out the member states, even though these soundings had been more cursory than usual in the case of the controversial finance package. Moreover, the Commission was only too aware that it had overplayed its hand on that occasion, and there was absolutely no doubt that it would be very much more cautious in future, with or without the external constraints of the Luxembourg Agreement.

On the major issue, of majority voting, the Luxembourg Agreement was anything but an agreement. The first paragraph of the statement issued after the meeting said that: 'When issues very important to one or more member countries are at stake, the members of the Council will try, within a reasonable time, to reach solutions which can be adopted by all the members of the Council.' But the second paragraph went on to say: 'The French delegation considers that, when very important interests are at stake, the discussion must be continued until unanimous agreement is reached.' Paragraph three added the obvious comment that there was a 'divergence of views' on what would happen if unanimous agreement was not reached, but paragraph four added soothingly that this divergence of views would not prevent the Community from resuming its activities. In practice, of course, there never had been any danger that one member country would be outvoted on an issue of vital national interest, and there was absolutely no reason to imagine that the move into the third stage of the transitional period on 1 January 1966 would change the situation in this respect. Nevertheless, the 1965

54

crisis and the Luxembourg confrontation certainly made the Five very much more hesitant to invoke the principle of majority voting on run-of-the-mill issues than they might otherwise have been.

So who had won? The Five had demonstrated a quite unusual degree of solidarity, and they left the battlefield undefeated in strictly legal terms, and the French had had to climb down a long way from the extreme demands set out by de Gaulle and Couve the previous autumn. The French had failed to secure formal agreement on any substantive modification of the institutional rules of the Community, and to that extent the French could be said to have lost. By precipitating the crisis General de Gaulle had given evidence of his alarm at the progress the Community was making, and the way in which economic integration in Europe was threatening to encroach on France's political independence – even though the most integrationist progress, on the farm policy, had all been achieved as the result of insistent pressure from Paris. But he had discovered that it was politically too late to change the rules, and economically too late to renounce the advantages of Common Market membership. He could resist the Commission's federalist package, but he could not turn the clock back.

Nevertheless, the French naturally claimed the Luxembourg Agreement as a massive victory for their point of view, and in the belief that Britain would in practice prove to be an ally in the majority voting controversy, immediately put out signals suggesting that the way was now open for the U.K. to join the Community. Two days after the Luxembourg Agreement, Olivier Wormser, the Economic Director at the Quai d'Orsay (subsequently Governor of the Bank of France), told me privately that 'majority voting is now dead', and predicted that the Six would very shortly invite Britain to join the Common Market. Similar views were being fed unofficially to Whitehall from other influential quarters in Paris, and the kite was flown more publicly a month later by Prince Jean de Broglie, French Deputy Foreign Minister, at a ministerial meeting of the Western European Union in London on 16 March 1966. He said that the French government thought it desirable that Britain should join and that talks should be resumed on the basis of the Rome Treaty. The difficulties would be less this time than they had been in 1961–3 and, he added, 'the prospects seem happy to us.'

At the time it was not at all clear how seriously the French government expected this new ploy to be taken. The French veto was barely two years old, the French attempt to rewrite the rules of the Community had only just been defeated, and it seemed imprudent to suppose that the General's fundamental aims had been transformed overnight. On the contrary, only a week earlier General de Gaulle had announced France's withdrawal from military integration in Nato, and two weeks later, on 29 March 1966, he gave notice that Nato's military H.Q. in Paris, as well as the American and Canadian troops stationed in France, had one year to leave. Having reclaimed French independent sovereignty in the European Community, he was now reclaiming it in the Atlantic Alliance; and to the extent that his attempt to eliminate economic integration had been formally defeated, he was all the more determined to eradicate military integration. (Nor was he to stop there: by the end of the year his policy of national independence was carried to its logical conclusion of neutralism, when the Chief of the Defence Staff, General Charles Ailleret, announced that in future French nuclear weapons would be targeted in all directions – *tous azimuths* – against the Americans as well as against the Russians.)

Against this background, his Common Market overtures to Britain were odd, to say the least. In the face of his Nato onslaught the British were proving the most energetic and committed members of the Alliance, acting in effect as the leaders in an intensive campaign to rally the thirteen other members round the principle of military integration, and treating French officers and diplomats at the Nato H.Q. in Paris as pariahs, if not actually as traitors. But it may have suited de Gaulle to play down the Nato conflict by offering an illusory Common Market olive branch to Britain and the Five; moreover, he still needed the good will of the Five in the forthcoming negotiations on farm finance and other agricultural regulations.

At all events, the British government decided that the French overtures should be taken seriously, if only to test their sincerity. At the conclusion of the W.E.U. meeting, Michael Stewart played up Jean de Broglie's remarks and announced that the French veto had now been lifted. During the election campaign that was now under way in Britain, Harold Wilson gradually and cautiously endorsed the idea of British membership, and after the Labour government was returned to power Michael Stewart announced that it would 'probe' the possibilities of reopening negotiations with the Six.

No decisive new move on the Common Market front was then made by the British government until November 1966, when Harold Wilson made a Declaration of Intent to explore the possibilities of Community membership. But in the meantime warming up of the Labour government's interest in Europe was matched by a parallel cooling of the French attitude. In early May 1966, at the Council of Europe in

Strasbourg, Jean de Broglie again spoke warmly of the French government's desire to see Britain join; but three weeks later Michel Debré, de Gaulle's hard-line Economics Minister, said that it would be difficult for Britain to join the Community for four or five years. In the meantime France had secured a new farm finance agreement. In July the Six agreed on the extension of price harmonization to beef, rice, milk, sugar and olive oil; when de Broglie next referred to the question of British membership, at W.E.U. in September, he merely emphasized all the difficulties it would create.

In principle the French had good reason to be satisfied with the progress made on the farm policy during 1966. The new finance agreement covered the entire period mid-1965 to end-1969, as the French government had always demanded, and the two questions which had sparked off the 1965 crisis — the powers of the Parliament and the Community's direct control over its own financial resources — were postponed until the end of the transitional period. For the first two years, the farm fund (F.E.O.G.A.) would be financed purely and simply by budgetary contributions from the member states according to fixed percentage keys; after the harmonization of prices on 1 July 1967, and for the rest of the transitional period, the fund would pay all the costs of the policy, and would receive ninety per cent of the income from food import levies. Any shortfall in the farm budget would be met by budgetary contributions from the member states (rather than from any revenue from industrial customs duties); and since the levy transfer would make Germany a much larger contributor than France, the French government accepted a slightly larger share in the balancing budgetary contribution (32 per cent) than Germany (31.2 per cent), while Holland, which would also be a net beneficiary under the farm policy, was to contribute slightly more (8.2 per cent) than Belgium (8.1. per cent). Luxembourg still stuck to 0.2 per cent, while the Italian share came down to 20.3 per cent, in recognition of its enormous increase in food imports.

Yet during 1965 and 1966 the French were becoming at heart increasingly disillusioned with the farm policy, which was inevitably failing to deal with the socio-economic problems of an inefficient, over-populated, fragmented farming sector, yet was creating new problems of its own in the shape of farm surpluses. The Community rules were too rigid to allow the French government to provide an adequate cushion for the poorer peasantry, and the finance bargaining on which the French government used up so much energy and so much good will in the end produced rather mediocre compensation. The harmonization of prices inevitably meant an increase in domestic French prices, and thus added to inflationary pressure; the French always protested that they did not want an increase in their own prices, but they knew it was pointless to expect German prices to come down more than half way. They insisted relentlessly on the harmonization of farm prices, because of their doctrinaire pursuit of the ideal of Community-wide free trade in farm products; yet within weeks of the common cereals price decision in December 1964 (which at the time was widely greeted as a great triumph), Olivier Wormser told me that the new price level was so high as to be 'silly'. And when in July 1965 the Six went on to fix common prices for other products, the French took a very sour view of their victory. After the meeting, Couve de Murville commented that the most important fact about the common agricultural policy was that it existed; the new decision made it much more difficult to defend the c.a.p. on economic grounds, because the prices fixed were much too high. 'There are two tragedies in life,' said Bernard Shaw. 'One is not to get your heart's desire. The other is to get it.'

Yet to secure these agreements on the farm policy, France had had to make concessions to the Five in other fields, notably in the conclusion of a special association agreement with Nigeria and in further progress in the Kennedy Round of international tariff-cutting negotiations which were in progress in Geneva. French objections to the Kennedy Round were the converse of German objections to common farm prices: French tariffs would in any case have to come down to the Community's average level (the common external tariff), and the Kennedy Round (which was intended to cut all industrial tariffs by fifty per cent) would mean still larger reductions in the effective protection for French industry. The Geneva negotiations had been going on since the spring of 1963, and the French boycott of the Community had meant a further six-month delay. But it was clear that they could not hold out for very much longer.

The French withdrawal from Nato in 1966 had its own drawbacks. On the political front General de Gaulle was able to assert France's status as one of the Big Four, by keeping French troops stationed in Germany even though they were no longer under Nato command; but he was obviously disappointed when the other members of Nato decided in October 1966 that the political Council and secretariat of the Alliance (of which France remained a member) should leave Paris and follow the military headquarters to Belgium. De Gaulle no doubt got considerable psychological satisfaction from the embarrassment he was causing to his allies and in particular to the Americans; but the departure of Nato and of the American troops inevitably meant a loss of foreign exchange, which would otherwise have been spent in France. In any case, General de Gaulle's withdrawal from Nato allowed the other members to undertake reforms which had long been blocked by French vetos, as Denis Healey, the British Defence Minister, was quick to point out. By the end of the year Healey and McNamara had set in motion the Nuclear Planning Group, to keep the European countries in closer contact with the Alliance's nuclear strategy, and Pierre Harmel, the new Belgian Foreign Minister, had been put in charge of wide-ranging studies on the best ways of adapting and enlarging the political and economic activities of the Alliance.

Wilson's Declaration of Intent to investigate the possibility of Britain joining the Common Market was met by a stony silence from the French government. The six foreign ministers discussed the British move on 22 December 1966 for the first time, but Couve remained coldly non-committal. Kurt Kiesinger, who had recently come to power in Germany at the head of a Grand Coalition of the two major parties, visited de Gaulle in Paris on 15 January 1967, but failed to persuade him to take a tolerant view of the British bid. The next day Harold Wilson and George Brown started out on their pilgrimage round the Common Market capitals, with the slogan 'We mean business'; but the French remained unimpressed. On 23 January, on the eve of his visit to Paris, Wilson delivered a rousing and emphatic speech on the importance of European integration to the Assembly of the Council of Europe, but when he got to Paris he found that, while he had captured the world's headlines, he had failed to make the smallest dent in French hostility.

The previous November Edouard de la Malène, a hard-line Gaullist deputy, had argued in the European Parliament that British entry would lead to the disintegration of the Community. In a television interview on the day after Wilson left Paris, Couve de Murville made much of all the economic and monetary difficulties which would be created by British entry, concentrating his fire on the problems raised by sterling's role as a reserve (or, as he put it, 'non-European') currency. Over the next ten months French government spokesmen rang the changes on these two themes, and used them as a justification for the second veto. The 'disintegration' argument was that an enlarged Community was bound to become a much looser grouping than the Six, and would gradually be absorbed into a 'vast free-trade area' including the United States. The advantage of this theme was that it could be played in two different keys – to keep Britain out or to weaken the rules of the Rome Treaty — and when he was playing this theme, Couve pretended to believe that the choice between a tight Community of six and a loose free-trade area of ten was a matter of complete indifference to his government.

The monetary argument was that Britain could not afford to join the Community so long as its balance of payments was in deficit, and could not be allowed to join so long as the pound was a reserve currency. The advantage of this argument was that France had succeeded in securing a farm finance agreement in the Community based on the principle that import levies would increasingly belong to the Community, and there was no getting away from the fact that the measures taken by the Wilson government in July 1966 had done little to eradicate Britain's serious balance of payments deficit. Opinion in the other capitals on the problems which might be caused by sterling's reserve role was sharply divided, but there were enough influential people (especially in the Commission) who agreed with the French to lend this aspect of the argument a certain amount of plausibility. After his talks with the Belgian government, for example, Wilson asserted roundly at a press conference: 'There are no doubts at all in Europe about sterling.' Yet everybody knew that the Belgians were concerned at the British balance of payments deficit, and two days later, on 3 February, Renaat van Elslande, the Belgian Deputy Foreign Minister, said that the position of sterling would have to be negotiated, together perhaps with the exchange rate of the pound, before Britain could enter. The doubters were joined a few days later by Jean Rey of the Commission, when he told the Institute of Banking in Paris that the pound's reserve role raised real difficulties.

Nevertheless, the British government continued to shuffle crab-wise towards a decision to ask for the reopening of negotiations with the Community. At the French general elections in the middle of March, the Gaullist party suffered a severe set-back and saw its majority cut to a sliver, and some people in London jumped to unwarranted conclusions. George Brown was imprudent enough to tell a meeting of Labour M.P.s on 6 April 1967 that de Gaulle was no longer influential enough to veto British membership: 'the General does not carry all that much support,' he said, 'even in his own country.' Three weeks later, at another Labour Party meeting, Harold Wilson came out firmly for British membership: 'I do believe that Europe could be on the verge of a great move forward in political unity, and that we can — and indeed must — play a part in it.' On 2 May, after a long and heated discussion in the cabinet, Wilson announced the government's decision to apply for negotiations; the next day, at a meeting of the French cabinet, General de Gaulle commented ominously that this 'is a very important matter which will no doubt take a considerable time to resolve.' A fortnight later, at his spring press conference, de Gaulle said that there never had been, and never would be, any question of a veto; but the obstacles to British membership were 'formidable'. He underlined all the economic problems: agricultural prices, agricultural financing, the British balance of payments deficit, capital movements, sterling's reserve role, the differences between Britain and the Six in the Kennedy Round, the differences between Britain and France over the reform of the international monetary system, Britain's 'special relationship' with the United States and her links with the Commonwealth. He proposed three alternative solutions: to admit Britain and her partners in Efta and thus turn the Community into a loose west Altantic free-trade area; to make all the Efta countries associate (i.e. second-class) members of the Community, without access to the decision-making institutions; or to wait for Britain to accomplish on her own the 'profound economic and political transformation which will enable her to join the European Community'. France would welcome such a historic conversion with all her heart, he said. George Brown had claimed that 'We expect to get in', but now there could be no serious grounds for optimism.

The battle over the British application started in earnest at the end of May, when the Six held a summit meeting in Rome ostensibly to celebrate the tenth anniversary of the signing of the Rome Treaty. De Gaulle demanded that the Six consider the matter very carefully, and that while they must certainly examine in detail all the concrete issues which would need to be covered in any negotiations, they must first hold 'profound and prolonged' discussions on the general problems which would be raised by the enlargement of the Community. For good measure, and to reinforce the divisions between the Five, he proposed that in the meantime the Six should start holding regular meetings to coordinate their foreign policies. No one could have been under the illusion that there was any prospect of de Gaulle coordinating his foreign policy with that of any other country, but the Germans had an insatiable appetite for this familiar French ploy, and the Italians as hosts of the summit were anxious that it should produce an agreement on something. De Gaulle's only determined adversary was Piet de Jong, the Dutch Prime Minister, who opposed any progress on political union between the Six until Britain should have joined the Community. None of the Five accepted the French argument that there must be a debate on the general principle of enlarging the Community, for the Rome

Treaty said explicitly that the Community should be open to other European countries. But there was no way of opening negotiations with the U.K. until the French agreed; they could hardly refuse to discuss the British application (even if they did not accept the French premise), and their only hope was to wear down the French government or prove that its 'anxieties' were baseless.

And so began the long, tedious months of argument. The first discussion on the British bid in the Council of Ministers was an empty exercise, since it coincided with the outbreak of the Six-Day War in the Middle East, and Couve, Brandt and Fanfani all stayed in their national capitals. Harold Wilson had a second meeting with General de Gaulle on 18 June, and though he told the House of Commons on his return 'I told him why we do not intend to take No for an answer', it was clear that he had made absolutely no impression on the French President. On 26 June, the six foreign ministers agreed that the Commission should prepare a report on the British application, but Couve vetoed the suggestion that the British government should be invited to make an opening statement to set out its negotiating position, and even forbade the Commission to have any contact with the British during the preparation of its report. The Five reluctantly agreed that at the next Council meeting there should be a discussion of the broad philosophical implications of enlarging the Community, but only on condition that there should also be a discussion of the concrete issues. A few days later the French government withdrew from the Anglo-French project to build a variable-geometry aircraft (A.F.V.G.), on the grounds of its cost; within weeks Avions Marcel Dassault had unveiled its own project for a swing-wing plane.

It was obvious, of course, that the French, the Five and the British were acting out a game of Diplomacy which could be no more than childish make-believe; yet they continued to play it in deadly earnest. Couve had no authority to forbid the Commission from meeting British diplomats accredited to the Community in Brussels and, above all, no way of enforcing his ban. George Brown sidestepped Couve's ban on an opening British statement, by making a long statement at the next ministerial meeting of the Western European Union, on 4 July in The Hague; André Bettencourt, the Deputy French Foreign Minister, attempted to prevent the statement from being 'accepted' by the Community institutions, but Joseph Luns, the Dutch Foreign Minister and chairman of the meeting, handed copies of the statement to Willy Brandt (the current chairman of the Council of Ministers of the Six) and to Jean Rey (the new President of the merged Commission), and announced that the statement had therefore been 'accepted' by the Community. With such debating points the summer passed, and General de Gaulle declared his support for the French-Canadian independence movement in Quebec.

While the British application remained deadlocked inside the Council of Ministers, progress was at last being made elsewhere on a reform of the international monetary system, and in particular on a plan for creating a new type of central bank currency called Special Drawing Rights. The United States had been arguing since the very early 1960s that the world's central banks were, or would very soon be, short of gold and foreign exchange reserves, and that some new form of reserve asset must therefore be created through the International Monetary Fund, in order to provide adequate liquidity to finance the rapid growth of world trade. General de Gaulle believed (not without some justification) that the main beneficiary of any artifically-created reserve asset would be the United States, and he had done his best to prevent any agreement in the negotiations which had started in 1962. In 1965 he had carried the war into the enemy camp by attacking the reserve currency system in general and the dollar in particular, and demanding that the world should return to an international payments system based simply on gold. The Five shared some of the French government's reservations about the reserve currency system and the facility with which it enabled the United States to run a balance of payments deficit, but they rejected the French recipe of a return to the gold standard, and in the last resort they accepted the American argument that a new form of reserve asset must, at some stage, be created to play a part alongside gold and foreign exchange. General de Gaulle had held up any progress for five years, but even he could not hold up progress for ever. By the summer of 1967 a compromise was beginning to emerge between the ten leading members of the International Monetary Fund, and the broad lines of the plan were endorsed at the Fund's annual meeting in Rio de Janeiro in September.

By the time of the Rio meeting, however, it was clear that Britain was in serious economic difficulty. The balance of payments was deteriorating sharply, the pound was under serious pressure in the foreign exchange markets, and the gold reserves were rapidly draining out of the Bank of England. It was becoming increasingly evident that a devaluation of the pound could not be averted for very much longer, though it was not generally considered good taste to say so in public.

No such economic prudery inhibited the Brussels Commission. The report on the British application, which it tabled on 2 October 1967, at a meeting of the Council of Ministers, argued that all of the concrete issues could be resolved through negotiations, and it accordingly recommended the opening of negotiations. So far so good. But the chapter on economic questions, which had been prepared under the supervision of Raymond Barre, a Gaullist professor who had recently joined the Commission from Paris, set out a damning indictment of the state of the British economy, included a broad hint that the pound ought to be devalued, and added that sterling could not continue to have a reserve role after Britain was inside the Community. With all the authority of its (comparatively) independent position as a Community institution, the Commission had provided an endorsement of all the French government's economic objections to British membership, and a cast-iron pretext for General de Gaulle to pronounce his veto.

Couve now felt that he could harden the French position still further. At this meeting, as well as at the next ding-dong battle between the Six on 23 October, he said that France would not agree to open negotiations with Britain until the British balance of payments was once more in surplus and the reserve role of the pound had been abandoned, and he echoed the Commission's broad hint that the pound ought to be devalued. The elimination of the British balance of payments deficit would obviously take several months, while the ending of the pound's reserve role would take several years and would require the cooperation not merely of all the sterling area countries but also of all the major industrialized countries to whom Britain owed money; Couve's two conditions meant postponing negotiations with Britain for a very long time indeed.

The French government consolidated its attack with a finely orchestrated series of leaks and inspired reports in the French press. On 9 October 1967, *Le Monde* reported that Britain was unable to meet $350 million of official debt repayments owed to the International Monetary Fund. On 13 November, after Britain had negotiated a $250 million credit from the Bank for International Settlement in Basle, in what had obviously become a last-ditch effort to avert devaluation, *Le Monde* reported that the U.K.'s short-term official debts had risen to $2,000 million. And in between it kept up a relentless barrage of adverse comment on the state of the British economy.

On the British side, the strain was beginning to tell. Towards the end of October reports appeared in the British press (subsequently traced to a Lausanne briefing given by Lord Chalfont, who was in charge of the Common Market bid), to the effect that Britain might have to reconsider its military alliances if negotiations were vetoed. The reports were immediately denied by Downing Street.

Two weeks later it was reported (this time by the B.B.C.) that Britain was again engaged in negotiating a large medium-term loan at a meeting of the Group of Ten in Paris. Questioned in the House of Commons on 15 November James Callaghan, the Chancellor of the Exchequer, would say only that it 'would be wrong either to confirm or deny a press rumour of this kind' – and turned the speculative pressures against the pound into a stampede. In fact the negotiations in Paris concerned not merely another large credit for Britain from the International Monetary Fund, but also the question of a devaluation of the pound. The British held out as long as they could, and the French made things as difficult as they could, but the struggle could not last for more than a few days. On 18 November 1967 the pound was devalued by 14.3 per cent, from \$2.80 to \$2.40, despite the fact that the I.M.F. credit had still not been finally negotiated.

If the British government believed that by devaluing it had met one of France's two conditions, and that the prospects for opening negotiations with the Community were thereby improved, it was sadly mistaken. Nine days later, in the ballroom of the Elysée Palace, General de Gaulle gave another of his dramatic press conferences. He again demanded a return to the gold standard; he reiterated his support for the break-away movement in Quebec; and he condemned the Israelis *(un peuple d'élite, sûr de lui-même et dominateur)* for the Six-Day War. But his major target was Britain. The Common Market was, he said, incompatible with the economy of Britain, whose balance of payments was in permanent disequilibrium and whose food came from overseas. It might be possible to imagine some sort of European free-trade area, but in that case it would be necessary to break up the Community and abolish its institutions. It was not possible to allow Britain to join the Community as it stood. *Et voilà, messieurs, dames.*

6 · The Second Veto and the Benelux Plan

By the time the gaunt old figure had disappeared behind the dark red curtains, it was clear that the British application was dead. But, as in 1963, it was still necessary to make sure that the death certificate was formally accepted by the other member states. Accordingly on 19 December, at yet another meeting of the Council of Ministers at the Kirchberg skyscraper in Luxembourg, Maurice Couve de Murville intoned all the familiar French arguments against the opening of membership negotiations with the British, and his colleagues bowed to the inevitable – only insisting that the communiqué should pin the responsibility unmistakably on France (as if there were any doubt of it). 'No member state,' it said, 'has raised any fundamental objection to the enlargement of the Communities .... One member state, however, expressed the opinion that this enlargement would profoundly alter the nature of the Communities, and the methods of administering them ...' It looked as though the body was now decently buried, whatever the regrets of some of the mourners.

The immediate reactions of the Five were only too predictable. Dr Joseph Luns immediately proclaimed to the waiting journalists that France had precipitated a new crisis in the Community. Jean Rey, President of the Commission, warned that it would create difficulties for the renegotiation of the Community's association agreement with France's former colonies in Africa, for the renegotiation of the Community's farm finance rules (from which France stood to gain), as well as for future relations with Spain, Algeria, Morocco and Tunisia (by which France set great store).

But Willy Brandt, the German Foreign Minister, refused to admit that the French veto could cause anything as severe as a crisis, and would only go on the record as saying that it would create 'problems'. The only moment of black comedy came when the Dutch abruptly walked out of a meeting of the six agriculture ministers (which was debating routine problems of the farm policy in a neighbouring room), in protest at the French veto: Edgar Faure, the French Agriculture Minister, plaintively murmured that he was personally wounded by such an act of discourtesy.

Couve himself remained completely unruffled by the anger of his partners. Strolling ostentatiously out of the Council chamber, he spent a good twenty minutes chatting easily to a group of journalists, his creased face radiating self-confidence and supercilious urbanity. Just why he went to so much trouble was not clear; he had nothing to gain personally by ingratiating himself with the world's press, since his career depended solely on the whim of one old man, and it was not his habit to fraternize with newspapermen; certainly, he had nothing to say that was new or illuminating – it was just another rehearsal of the well-worn phrases. Perhaps he was feeling that, the second time around, a veto on British membership had become not merely a professional duty but even a personal pleasure; or perhaps again, he may have been worried that it might not, after all, be quite so easy to carry off this time as in 1963. I could not tell then, and I do not know now; all I do know is that at the time it was a nauseating spectacle of false bonhomie.

Even if Couve did have a few residual anxieties, it seemed probable that afternoon in Luxembourg that the French would get away with it, as they had done so often in the past. The communiqué recalled only too vividly the terms of the Luxembourg Agreement of January 1966, and if the Community had been able to survive a seven-month French boycott, it could surely survive a second veto on British membership. If the experience of the first veto was anything to go by, there would be three months of bitterness and bickering, with the Dutch doing their best to make difficulties for anything that might interest the French. Token efforts would be made to keep the British question in the forefront of the Community's agenda, if not in terms of membership, then at least in some other symbolic way. The Germans would laboriously and (it must be said) stupidly attempt to find a compromise between the French and Dutch points of view, and would lumber down every blind alley marked out for them by the Quai d'Orsay. But after a while, they would all get tired of the hopeless task of trying to get General de Gaulle to change his mind, and the Community would gradually revert to its real business of making economic concessions to France.

That seemed the most plausible scenario. Events turned out subtly, but significantly different. The Dutch did indeed embark on a systematic process of obstruction, at least over questions which were not obligatory under the Rome Treaty, for example over advanced technology. The French had been pressing for more technological cooperation between the Six, but outside the Community and on a non-integrated, à la carte basis; the Dutch now refused to take any further part in these discussions unless they were enlarged to include the United Kingdom.

The Germans too acted precisely as one might have expected, with long-winded and elaborate proposals for some form of 'pre-membership' through tariff-cutting, in the ridiculous hope that a formula could be found which would satisfy both the French and the British. In reality there could be no such formula, since the British were only interested in full membership, and that was the one thing which the French were not prepared to allow. Time and again, with pathetic seriousness, the Germans redrafted their proposals; time and again the French projected the mirage of compromise a little further off; time and again the Germans went home disappointed but undeterred.

At every moment it seemed as if the French had finally succeeded in wearing their partners down, and that at the next meeting of the Council of Ministers the weary ghost of the British application would be laid to rest for ever. Yet the next meeting came, and still the problem refused to lie down, still the Five returned with new proposals, still the argument ground on. I suppose I must have mentally written off the British question half a dozen times in the course of 1968, and each time I was wrong. In fact, it did not cease to hang over the Six until the French finally agreed in December 1969 — two years after the second veto — to open negotiations with the U.K. By that time, of course, a great deal had changed: General de Gaulle had been nearly toppled from power by the May Revolution, the French economy had been blown right off course, the international monetary system had been shaken by a series of violent currency crises (with the French franc and the common agricultural policy as leading victims), the Russians had crushed the Czechs, and General de Gaulle had himself withdrawn from the Elysée into his last, short-lived retirement.

But the crucial factor which really tipped the scales against the French was none of these headline-catching events. It was a modest little proposal put forward by the Dutch, with the support of the Belgians and the Luxembourgers, called the Benelux Plan. The fact that the Benelux Plan never got off the ground as it stood is neither here nor there. It represented the first direct and considered political challenge to General de Gaulle's leadership of the Community, and as such it had to be taken seriously.

The content of the plan was vague and apparently innocuous. The three Benelux countries simply proposed to embark on regular consultations on foreign policy, and they invited other European countries (including those outside the Community) to join them; any country which took part would have to undertake always to consult its partners before taking foreign policy decisions, though it would not be obliged to fall in with their views. And that essentially was all. There was no question of unanimity or majority voting, no supranationality, no link with the Rome Treaty or the Community.

The implications of the proposal were dynamite in Paris, however, precisely because it was so modest and reasonable. The Beneluxers were not threatening reprisals against France, nor were they attempting to destroy the Community. They were not even setting out to exclude France from participating in their new plan; on the contrary, France was welcome to join in. But they were proposing to set up what amounted to a new institution outside and above the Community, where the Community rules and in particular the French veto would no longer operate. It was generally agreed, even by people of widely differing views, that the process of European integration ought, at some time or other, to lead to political unification, starting no doubt with the coordination of foreign policies. It was indeed a bait which General de Gaulle had frequently held out to the Five, either as a way of undermining the rules of the Community (as in the 1961−2 Fouchet negotiations) or as a way of luring them away from other pre-occupations (as at the 1967 Rome Summit). But the Rome Treaty itself did not include any specific mention of political union, and the Benelux countries were therefore fully entitled to propose the participation of all European countries, including the U.K.

In other words, though the Luxembourg Agreement had reinforced France's veto power inside the Community, it could not operate against the Benelux Plan, and the institutional rules which General de Gaulle had successfully used to keep Britain out of the Common Market on two occasions could not be brought into play against the new gambit from the Low Countries. This point, which was evident from the plan itself, was explicitly brought out by the Dutch and Belgian foreign ministries in their background briefings on the plan. They were tired of finding that their loyalty to the rules of the Community was repeatedly used against them, and they were now determined to form a new grouping which would rise above the E.E.C. France was invited to take part, just like any other member of the Community, but France would have no power to prevent the formation of the new grouping, and in particular could not prevent Britain from joining it. The Beneluxers maintained that nothing would be done to infringe on the prerogatives of the Community, and no doubt they meant it. But it was evident that, if the plan did in fact lead to an effective coordination of foreign policies, it would in time become a political court of appeal in Europe, and would have a preponderant influence over anything decided in the European Economic Community. The irony of the Benelux Plan was that it precisely recalled the French Fouchet Plan of 1961−2, by which General de Gaulle had tried to over-ride the supranational implications of the Community, by capping it with an inter-governmental committee of foreign ministers. The one essential difference, of course, was that the Fouchet Plan was confined to the Six.

At least as important as the content of the plan was its sponsorship. The French had learned to expect the energetic hostility of the Dutch, but they had not expected that the Dutch would be able to enlist the whole-hearted support of the Belgians and the Luxembourgers. Though about half Belgium's population is Flemish, its business community and its cultural interests have long been oriented towards France, and its foreign policies have tended to be either openly pro-French or at least on the fence between Paris and the rest. Tiny Luxembourg is even less well-endowed for conducting an independent foreign policy, and has usually preferred to steer clear of any major clash with the bigger Community countries. At the personal level, too, the Benelux initiative was striking. Paul-Henri Spaak, the former Belgain Foreign Minister, was a rumbustious character with a tendency to fly off the handle, but not very much firmness of purpose. Pierre Harmel, his successor at the rue des Quatre Bras in Brussels, was a mild, soft-spoken man, with little talent for theatrical gestures; if he was prepared to stand up to the French the challenge must be serious.

At the time, however, it was not at all evident that the Benelux Plan would have a decisive influence on the course of events. It kept re-appearing in such a variety of forms that it was sometimes difficult to be sure that it was still the same plan. In any case, the plan would only be successful if it attracted the support of some of the big countries inside the Community, and it was far from certain that Germany or Italy would be prepared to throw in their lot against France. It was even difficult to feel confident, amidst the swirl of diplomatic comings and goings during the early weeks of 1968, that the three Benelux countries would have the strength of purpose to stick to their plan.

The British government's attitude to the plan was a foregone conclusion. When the Benelux countries made their announcement on 15 January, it was immediately welcomed by the U.K. This was not surprising, since the Beneluxers had taken the precaution of sounding out the British beforehand and of tailoring it to suit them, and they did not release it until they were sure of a welcome from London. Within three weeks London's approving noises had been echoed by Denmark, Norway and Sweden – which in Sweden's case was rather presumptuous, since their self-imposed neutrality prevented them from seeking full membership in the Community and must presumably prevent them from joining a European foreign policy union too.

Inside the Community, the reactions from the other national capitals were diverse but, on the whole, discouraging. The French were shocked into silence, but unmistakably hostile. The Italians were uncertain, and could not be counted upon to come out into the open, though they did support the Dutch in a number of other, minor reprisals against the French. The Germans refused to commit themselves to the Benelux Plan, because they wanted to launch a plan of their own. Jean Rey of the Commission publicly condemned any attempt to create new institutions outside the rules of the Rome Treaty, no doubt because he felt it would be a slur on the position of the Commission. Instead he proposed some face-saving innovations, including a strengthening of the Association agreement between the U.K. and the European Coal and Steel Community, discussions with the U.K. on its economic problems (as if in compensation for its damning report the previous October?), and 'a certain number of common actions', which remained unspecified because they were unspecifiable. Three weeks later, however, he exposed himself as an inconstant weathercock, by coming out in support of the Benelux Plan.

The fate of the plan lay in Bonn. If the Germans threw their weight behind it, it was more than likely that the Italians would come off the fence, and the plan would immediately become politically viable, leaving only the French in the uncomfortable dilemma between joining in or staying out. In theory the Germans were already tied to a special relationship with France, by the 1963 Franco-German Friendship Treaty, and though the political differences between Paris and Bonn were deep, manifold and obvious, the Germans were reluctant to take a step which could only be interpreted as a rejection of the Treaty and all that it implied. They tried to avoid the choice by looking for some middle road which would satisfy both London and Paris.

This middle way, as conceived by the German Foreign Minister, Willy Brandt, was a plan to bring Britain into the Community by stages.

The first stage would be free trade between Britain and the Six, the second stage an economic and customs union, and the third stage full membership. After George Brown visited Bonn on 19 January 1968, when the Benelux Plan was only four days old, he no longer had much hope of being able to sell it to the Germans, since they seemed irrevocably wedded to their own scheme.

Yet one did not need to be a clairvoyant to see that, whatever the ultimate fate of the Benelux Plan, the Brandt Plan was doomed to fail. For the British there would be obvious attractions in securing tariff-free access to the Community market for industrial goods, but in political terms the Wilson government had no intention of accepting what would amount to second-class citizenship of the new Europe, even for a limited period. For the French there could be no economic advantage in allowing Britain free access to the Common Market, unless Britain paid a heavy entrance fee by contributing in some way to the common agricultural policy. But that in turn would reduce Britain's advantage in joining the industrial free-trade area, and there could be no prospect of her agreeing to support the farm policy if she had no right to take part in shaping it. But the French would inevitably oppose any British share in policy-making, since it would represent an irreversible step towards full membership in all other areas of the Community's work. In short, for a country of Britain's size and importance, there could be no half-way house between membership and non-membership, and everybody knew it, except the Germans.

The French government encouraged the Germans in their illusions, in order to distract them from the Benelux Plan, but at successive meetings, while appearing to endorse the German proposals in principle, sliced away at them until there was nothing left.

Nevertheless, General de Gaulle found it expedient to make pacific gestures to his Common Market partners, if only on marginal issues. On 22 January Maurice Couve de Murville appeared on German television to say that European unity depended on Franco-German cooperation, and that Germany had moved closer to France on Europe's major problems. This was very different stuff from de Gaulle's habitual denunciations of Bonn's back-sliding, and it was not even true; but it must have seemed politic to say it. Unfortunately Willy Brandt, appearing on French television that very same night, underlined the important political differences between their two countries, and pointed out that there was no hope of political cooperation in Europe until the enlargement of the Community had been agreed. France and Germany, he said, are no substitute for the Community.

The next day Jean de Lipkowski, a minor Gaullist politician, launched the idea of pre-membership for Britain, with trade liberalization, the alignment of Britain's farm policy on that of the Community, and a consultative council between Britain and the Six — but with no automatic guarantee of ultimate full membership. This ostensibly constructive proposal was followed by a more concrete concession to British interests on 8 February, when the French government started to back away from its tough opening position on the request of Kenya, Tanzania and Uganda for association with the Community. Hitherto the French had been blocking the East African negotiations, by insisting that any trade concessions offered by the Community must be paid for in full by matching concessions from the African countries; now the French agreed to soften their demand for full reciprocity. They also agreed that any technological projects adopted by the Six should be open to British participation.

In the middle of February Chancellor Kurt Kiesinger visited Paris, and, as on so many other occasions, the German delegation was hoodwinked; partly by the wiles of the General, partly by their own determination to perceive agreement where no agreement could possibly exist. Kiesinger emerged from his talks at the Elysée apparently convinced that de Gaulle had agreed to back some (unspecified) trading arrangement on industrial and agricultural products between the Community and the four candidate countries (Britain, Norway, Denmark and Ireland). As a proof of his good will, the German Chancellor agreed to defer a decision on the Benelux Plan, and as a proof of *his* good will, the French President pronounced himself in favour of the enlargement of the Community — 'as soon as these countries should be in a position effectively to enter the Community, or to form other links with it.'

Kurt Kiesinger had been elected partly in the hope that he would be able to mend Franco-German relations, which had deteriorated severely under his predecessor Ludwig Erhard, and he returned home to Bonn thoroughly satisfied with his achievement in Paris. But five days later Harold Wilson in the House of Commons, and Piet de Jong in the Dutch Lower House, both declared roundly that the Paris Declaration could be no substitute for the Benelux Plan, while Jean Rey in Brussels argued (absurdly) that the Benelux Plan and the Paris Declaration should both form part of a package deal with the U.K.

When Willy Brandt next saw Couve de Murville, in the Council of Ministers on 29 February, he began to discover just how illusory the Paris agreement had been. He proposed steep across-the-board reductions in industrial customs duties between Britain and the Six, and implied that all duties should be eliminated within three to five years. He found, however, that the French were in no hurry to agree to a tariff-cutting plan, and especially not a tariff-cutting plan on this scale; the only thing they were clear about was that under any trading arrangement Britain must undertake to buy fixed quantities of (French) farm surpluses. Ten days later the six foreign ministers met again in Brussels to grind through the arguments once more, with little or no result; except that this time Couve announced that France could only agree to very limited tariff cuts, and for a limited period, and with absolutely no question of a free-trade area, a customs union, or anything else that smacked of full membership.

And so it went on, week after week. Brandt visited Paris again on 22 April, and Couve graciously agreed to his request that there should be yet another meeting of the Council to discuss the question of a trading arrangement with Britain; but he gave him no reason to believe that the French government would be any more forthcoming in the future than it had been in the past.

At the next regular meeting of Western European Union, Michael Stewart, the new British Foreign Secretary, told the Six that Britain was still determined to press for full membership of the Community, was not interested in any substitute for membership, and would only consider proposals from the Six if they were unmistakably linked to full membership. Willy Brandt said Stewart's statement made him 'very happy', Pierre Harmel said it was 'very important', and the Italians characteristically announced that it had given them 'great joy'. But the cause of British membership was not one whit further forward.

One could go on, tracing the minutiae of the debate between Bonn and Paris during the ensuing months, with the Germans gradually reducing their proposal to a modest thirty per cent cut in tariffs, with the French each time offering slightly less, and with the Benelux countries impatiently waiting for the Germans to recognize the hopelessness of going on, and at last to take a decision on the Benelux Plan. But though the six foreign ministers ground relentlessly away in their interminable and sterile debates on the British question all through the spring and summer, their arguments were soon over-shadowed, first by a new outbreak of the international monetary crisis, and then even more dramatically by the May Revolution in France.

When it came, it was obvious that the May Revolution represented a serious blow to General de Gaulle's authority in France, and therefore to his capacity for free-wheeling destructiveness abroad. It only gradually became apparent that the monetary whirlwind which he had done so much to conjure up — with his repeated demands for a return to the gold standard, with his constant attacks on the dollar and the reserve currency system, and with his ruthless campaign against the pound — would inflict the worst damage on France.

7 · Gold Rush

During the autumn of 1967, the weakness of the pound had been the focal point of the international monetary disturbances, though the rush to sell pounds and buy gold had reached a level which was starting to put strains on the entire monetary system. In normal circumstances the sterling devaluation might have been expected to bring the British balance of payments back into surplus and restore calm to the foreign exchange markets. But these were not normal circumstances, and calm did not return, nor Britain climb out of the red, until the international monetary system had passed through its most serious crisi; since the war.

In the first place, the circumstances of the British devaluation were highly unfavourable. The French continued their sniping tactics even after the devaluation had been announced, and spread press reports that the U.K. was having serious difficulty in arranging the necessary $1,400 million stand-by credit from the International Monetary Fund, and that an increase in the official price of gold was imminent. The Paris negotiations had been conducted in such an atmosphere of crisis and mistrust, that it was impossible for anyone to believe that all would be sweetness and light from now on. Henry Fowler, the U.S. Secretary of the Treasury, was honest (and unwise) enough to say publicly that the dollar was now 'in the front line'. Finally, if James Callaghan had made a palpable mess of carrying out the devaluation, his successor at the Treasury, Roy Jenkins, seemed to be making an even bigger mess of making it work. He delayed taking the necessary deflationary measures to back up the devaluation until the normal spring budget, four months later, and this delay may well help to account for the extreme slowness with which Britain's external account got back into balance.

It was hardly surprising, therefore, that speculation against the dollar and the pound, and demand for gold, soared to new record heights in the closing weeks of 1967, and remained intense during the early months of 1968. The United States reasserted several times both on its own account and in conjunction with the other leading industrial countries, that the price of gold would remain at its official level of $35 an ounce. But in those dizzy days of mingled ecstasy and panic, the gold rush had acquired a momentum of its own, and was pushing the entire international monetary system into a position of dangerous uncertainty. In theory, the United States was in a position to decide what price it would pay for gold, and what price it would take for it, and legally this decision rested with Congress. In practice the Americans were engaged in a vast game of bluff with the speculators – and, incidentally, with the other central banks in Europe and Japan. They were committed to the principle of selling gold for dollars at a price of $35 an ounce, but their gold stock was not nearly large enough to buy back, *at this price,* all the dollars held by foreign central banks, let alone all the dollars held privately abroad. In the last resort, the U.S. Treasury could simply close the gold-sales window, or alternatively sell off every last bar of gold in exchange for dollars, and then challenge the rest of the world to see if they could do without the dollars they had accumulated. If the Americans were to adopt either of these extreme courses, it seemed virtually certain that the position of the dollar as the world's dominant currency would be immeasurably strengthened, just because of the overwhelming importance of the American economy. From time to time, indeed, the U.S. Treasury did drop veiled hints that it was prepared to take the drastic step of banishing gold from any effective role in the international monetary system, but it was clear that Washington was anxious to avoid going to this extremity, if at all possible. The calculation in the minds of the speculators was that, in the last analysis, the American administration would prefer to raise the price of gold, and thus give the buyers of gold a handsome profit.

The chief reason for their confidence was that, when they bought gold, they were in practice buying it from the major central banks, and principally from the United States, through the price-stabilizing mechanisms of the so-called Gold Pool. The Gold Pool had been set up in 1960 by Britain and America to keep the price of gold on the free market at or very close to the official price of $35 an ounce, and they were joined a year later by the central banks of France, Germany, Italy, Switzerland, Holland and Belgium. Since London was the world's leading free gold market, the Bank of England acted as agent for its partners in the Pool, and bought gold whenever the price dropped below $35, and sold it whenever the price rose above $35. Each of the central banks contributed in a fixed proportion, with the United States taking half of the gold that was bought by the Pool, and providing half the gold that was sold by it.

In the early years, the supply of new gold coming on to the market was greater than the demand, and the eight central banks were able to take the surplus, in amounts which varied between $220 million and $840 million every year. But after General de Gaulle launched his campaign for a return to the gold standard in 1965, private demand rose steeply, while the Soviet Union (hitherto one of the major sources of supply after South Africa) abruptly ceased selling any gold on the free market. Perhaps the Russians were making a gesture of political solidarity with General de Gaulle against the United States, or perhaps they simply believed that his campaign would bring them a commercial advantage. Whatever their reasons, they helped to tilt the balance against the Gold Pool, which started losing gold in 1965.

By the closing weeks of 1967, the drain on the gold stocks of the Gold Pool participants had swelled from a trickle to a flood, and the French government was making things a good deal worse for its partners than they would otherwise have been. On the one hand, the French government was converting its own dollars directly into gold at the Federal Reserve Bank in New York. On the other hand, it was also stimulating speculative buying by private individuals by its propaganda campaign (thus adding to the drain on the American gold reserves), and indirectly intensifying the anxieties of the other central banks about the gold-convertibility of *their* dollar holdings. At the same time, however, the Banque de France was also losing gold through its participation in the Gold Pool. It was only logical, therefore, that the French would decide to protect themselves against the backlash of their propaganda, by withdrawing from the Gold Pool; when they did withdraw, in June 1967, their share in the Pool, of just over nine per cent, had to be taken over by someone else – and almost inevitably it had to be taken over by the United States. Naturally, this only exacerbated the gold haemorrhage from the United States; and when the French deftly leaked the news of their defection from the Gold Pool, just after the sterling devaluation, in an article in *Le Monde* the frenzy on the gold market knew no bounds.

The frenzy was only increased by the futile attempts of the Americans and their partners to restore order. Immediately after the sterling devaluation Washington restated the immutability of the $35 price, and a few days later a similar statement was issued jointly by all the remaining members of the Gold Pool. On 10 December, the Gold Pool countries met in Basle, but on this occasion made no public statement; and if their words had been greeted with derision, their silence was taken as evidence that the managers of the international monetary system were on the run.

On 1 January, President Johnson launched a massive new programme to improve the American balance of payments. But though it created quite a stir, it came too late to affect the underlying premise of the gold speculators, which was that the American gold reserves were far too low to meet the pressure of dollar conversion. In one respect, it also provided ammunition for the Gaullist opponents of British membership of the European Community; for while Johnson introduced severe new restrictions on overseas investment by American companies, these restrictions were far more severe on investment on the continent of Europe than in Britain, and this was cited by the Gaullist organ *La Nation* as a further proof of Britain's privileged position in Washington.

By the middle of March 1968 it was clear that more drastic action was needed to stem the gold rush. In the four months that had elapsed since the devaluation of the pound, the seven-member Gold Pool had lost over $3,000 million worth of gold, and further losses at this rate could not be borne. Accordingly, yet another meeting of the Pool was convened on 16 and 17 March, in Washington, and this time they did take effective action. They announced that they would no longer provide any gold to the free market, that the Gold Pool would cease operations forthwith, and that while the United States remained ready to sell gold to central banks, it would not sell gold to any central banks which provided gold for the free market. As a rationalization for their action, they announced that the official international monetary system no longer had any need of additional supplies of gold in its reserves, with the obvious implication that gold would no longer be at the centre of the system. But the real meaning of their decision was that in future there would be two types of gold, which would be kept rigorously separate; one for central banks and one for private uses. The question immediately raised by the Washington statement was: Can they make it stick?

Certainly, the odds against the new official gold policy seemed weighted against the Americans and their partners. General de Gaulle had, of course, not been consulted (since France was no longer in the Gold Pool), and his fulminations against the Washington decision were only as vehement as might have been expected. Of considerably more consequence was the announcement by the South African government that it would no longer sell any of its newly-mined gold on the free market. South Africa is by far the largest gold producer in the free world, and Pretoria had long supported the French campaign for an increase in the official gold price. If South African gold were kept out of the market, the price would be sure to rise, perhaps in quite dramatic proportions, and might even reach the point where the gap between the free market price and the official $35 price maintained by the United States was so large that the two-tier system would break down. For at some point the incentive for the smaller central banks to take advantage of the inflated free price would become so large that they would find ways round the American ban, and Washington would once more be faced with the choice between an increase in the official price – and even more draconian exchange controls on the outflow of gold.

To begin with, these arguments seemed likely to be proved right. The price on the free market shot up immediately after the closing of the Gold Pool, to $40 an ounce, and then oscillated violently between $37 and $40, and, after the outbreak of the May Revolution in France, it rose once more to almost $43 an ounce. But in the medium-term, at any rate, the dice were loaded against the South African tactic, because South Africa was already in the red in its trade with the rest of the world, and could not long afford to be without the foreign income provided by its sales of gold. As the months passed, and still the gold price failed to rise anywhere near the levels advocated by the French and the South Africans, it gradually came to be accepted that the gamble of the Americans and their partners might after all pay off. Towards the end of 1968, and throughout 1969, the free market price subsided with the hopes of the spectulators, not least because a significant proportion of them had bought gold on borrowed money, which at that time was costing them very high rates of interest. At the same time, 1968 was also a boom period for a number of the biggest international stock markets, including Wall Street, Tokyo, Sydney, London and Johannesburg, and a good many of the speculators saw better prospects of making money in shares than in gold bars – even if some of the shares were those of gold mining companies in South Africa.

By the end of 1969, Dr Diederichs, the South African Finance Minister, had to cry peace and settle for an agreement with Washington which forced South Africa to sell most of its gold on the free market whenever the price there was above $35 an ounce. In the weeks following the Pretoria–Washington agreement, it appeared that the American victory was complete, for the free gold price remained either at $35 an ounce or very close to it, and was more often below than above. A year later, in 1971, the price had again started to move

80

upwards, but that is another story.

In the purely European context, the closing of the Gold Pool in March 1968 was evidently a serious diplomatic reverse for General de Gaulle. Only time was to show that the new policy could be made to work, but the Five had demonstrated that, if they were forced to choose between Paris and Washington, they would come down, however reluctantly, on the side of Washington. It was not that they regarded the American balance of payments deficit with easy-going complacency, or believed that the United States had a God-given right to run the international monetary system in whatever way was convenient to its national interest. But they could see no good coming out of an international monetary war, and no point in trying to reverse the dominating role of the dollar until some agreement should be reached on something to put in its place. This was what divided them from the French. Out of a fatalistic despair, or perhaps because he considered the technical monetary problems to be nothing more than part of the visible tip of a more pervasive political reality, General de Gaulle was only interested in the lonely exaltation of an unequal war; so unequal was it, that to negotiate was to be defeated.

Willy-nilly, he was already in the process of being dragged into two other economic negotiations with the United States, with his Common Market partners as very undependable allies. With his balance of payments programme announced on 1 January, Lyndon Johnson appeared to be making a serious, if belated attempt to bring America's payments in balance with the rest of the world. In recognition of this fact, several European countries offered to make the process easier for the Americans by accelerating the tariff cuts which they had agreed to make in the Kennedy Round. The most generous offer was that made by Anthony Crosland in the House of Commons on 14 March, which would have crammed three of the five annual tariff cuts into two years. This proposal would not have increased the depth of the tariff cuts at the end of the five-year period, but it would have given the Americans a temporary advantage by implementing the European tariff cuts rather more quickly in the early years than the American ones.

Naturally, the French were hostile to any such good-will gesture towards the United States, partly on political grounds, but partly because they had their own difficulties. In the process of creating their customs union, the Six had not merely to eliminate all tariffs on trade between themselves, but also to harmonize their tariffs on imports from outside the Common Market at a single level, known as the common external tariff. But since the French, like the Italians, had always been much more protectionist than the relatively free-trading Dutch and Germans, their national tariffs started off at a much higher level than theirs. Now 1 July 1968 had been fixed as the date for completing the E.E.C. customs union, which meant that France and Italy would not only have to remove their remaining customs duties on imports from other Common Market countries, but would also have to bring their customs duties on imports from outside the Common Market down to the level of the common external tariff. And since the Six were already committed to making these tariff changes in any case, they had decided for simplicity's sake to incorporate at the same time two of the five Kennedy Round slices; whereas the Americans had made one of the five cuts at the beginning of 1968 and would make the second at the beginning of 1969, and so on. Thus for the French to accept an acceleration in the Kennedy Round cuts would expose them to rather a sudden increase in competition from foreign manufacturers, and it was not surprising that they were hostile to the whole idea.

General de Gaulle was beginning to perceive, however, that he couldn't hope to win on all fronts at once by himself, and that he must give ground on some minor questions if he was to make progress on major ones. In political terms the acceleration of the Kennedy Round tariff cuts was, in the long run, only a minor issue, since the balance agreed in Geneva would have been restored before the five years were up. The establishment of a new international reserve asset in the International Monetary Fund, on the other hand (in the form of Special Drawing Rights) was obviously a major issue, since it involved permanent changes in the operation of the international monetary system. Negotiations on this issue were obviously entering their decisive phase, since the details of the broad scheme adopted at Rio by all members of the I.M.F. the previous autumn were scheduled to be hammered out at a ministerial meeting of the Group of Ten in Stockholm on 29 March.

So when the Council of Ministers of the Six met in Brussels on 25 March to argue about an acceleration of the Kennedy Round cuts, the French had a bargaining weapon against the Five. The Germans, the Dutch and the Italians all supported the British proposal, while the Commission, no doubt in search of a compromise, proposed a rather smaller acceleration in European cuts, to be off-set by a slow-down in the pace of America's own tariff cuts. The French turned down both suggestions, ostensibly because the United States had not done enough to put its own house in order, by abolishing protectionist trading measures and adopting a tougher economic policy at home; in reality because this enabled Paris to postpone any decision until after the Stockholm meeting of the Group of Ten four days later.

In Stockholm, Michel Debré, France's Finance Minister, launched into a passionate and desperate onslaught on the Special Drawing Rights proposals, with unrestrained briefings for any journalist who cared to listen and hysterical declamations inside the negotiating chamber. He maintained that the whole scheme had been distorted out of all recognition since the annual meeting of the International Monetary Fund in Rio de Janeiro the previous autumn. He insisted that the use of the new reserve instrument must be circumscribed with much greater restrictions. Above all, he demanded that the scheme should be put into cold storage until there should have been a profound re-examination of the entire international monetary system, which he said was rotten to the core and ought to be replaced by a new system based entirely on gold and credit.

If Debré had adopted slightly less hysterical tactics, it is possible that he would have secured additional concessions on the rules governing the new Special Drawing Rights, but it rapidly became clear that he was not doing the French cause any good at all by throwing a tantrum. Many of the other ministers present could agree that there was something seriously wrong with the international monetary system, and some of them said so. But none of them could agree that this was the right moment to scrap the results of five years of negotiations and start all over again. The Germans and the Italians attempted, as they had so often in the past, to find some middle ground between the French and the Americans. They gave up the attempt when they found, once more, that the French were not interested in the middle ground, and the solidarity of the Six, not naturally a strong plant at the best of times, withered and died.

By the closing day of the Stockholm conference, Michel Debré had two options: to back down or to walk out. It was entirely consistent with the Gaullist record and with his performance at the conference that he should have chosen to walk out, in a metaphorical sense: he told the other ministers that France would not take part in the Special Drawing Rights scheme. It was a powerful last card. As a completely new form of reserve asset, Special Drawing Rights would depend heavily for their credibility on the readiness of all or virtually all the big countries to accept them in exchange for gold or currencies. By refusing to participate, France could weaken the S.D.R. scheme, just as she had weakened Nato by walking out of the military side of that organization. But it was not a fatal threat, provided no other major country followed suit. In Stockholm, all the other members of the Group of Ten endorsed the scheme, and its adoption by the wider forum of the full membership of the International Monetary Fund was virtually a foregone conclusion. Significantly, France did not even gain the support of all her client states in the Franc Zone in Africa, who could see no valid reason why they should forego what amounted to a free distribution of cash for the sake of General de Gaulle's increasingly extreme views on the way the world should be organized. At the I.M.F. meeting in Washington that autumn, the S.D.R. scheme was duly passed, without French approval – though by that time General de Gaulle was in such trouble at home that it was evident that he, or his successors, would be only too glad to subscribe to it after all.

8 · May Revolution

The May Revolution must surely go down as one of the most extraordinary eruptions of political protest in the post-war period. Extraordinary by its suddenness and unexpectedness, extraordinary for the flowering of ecstasy which it engendered, extraordinary for the wholly unpremeditated way in which a student demonstration sparked off a national strike and almost led to the collapse of what had been widely considered the strongest regime of any democratic country.

By the late sixties, student protests were commonplace in most universities throughout the western world, from Tokyo to Berlin and from the London School of Economics to Berkeley. But the French student protest movement, which transferred its attentions from the Nanterre campus in the suburbs of Paris to the Sorbonne in the centre of the city on 3 May 1968, was the only one to trigger off disturbances on a truly national scale. On that Friday night the students had their first large-scale clash with the police, and a week later, on the Night of the Barricades (Friday, 10 May), over 360 people were wounded. On the Monday the trade unions staged a mass demonstration in favour of the students with a rally of over three quarters of a million of their followers. On the Tuesday the first strike broke out quite spontaneously, within a matter of days the strike had spread like an epidemic, and by the end of a fortnight over nine million workers had walked out of, or occupied, their factories.

Just why the student movement was able to unleash a national strike is still something of a mystery. No one who was in Paris at the time could fail to recognize the mood of exhilaration. For the first time in ten years General de Gaulle's authority was being effectively challenged, for the first time in ten years the French people were feeling the exaltation and the anxiety of an uncertain future, for the first time in living memory the Parisians (who are normally far more reserved, if not actually hostile, towards their fellow-men than any Englishman could ever be), found themselves engaging in spontaneous and animated political discussions with perfect strangers at bus stops and Metro stations. Perhaps inevitably, the sympathy of *les bons bourgeois* for the students faded away after too many of their cars had been burned in barricade battles between the students and *les sales flics*. But by that time the student movement was overshadowed by the industrial strike, which had acquired an uncontrolled and spontaneous momentum of its own.

The very scale of the strike showed that it was prompted by far deeper currents of discontent than simple dissatisfaction with wages or working conditions. From start to finish it remained leaderless and unorganized, in defiance of all the official trade union bodies, and if in the end the strikers agreed to return to work, in return for a very large increase in wages, that was only because they could see no prospect of securing any more fundamental improvement in their lot. The all-night talkathons of the students at the Sorbonne and the Théâtre de l'Odéon failed to produce any viable alternative to existing social and political institutions, and the workers had wives and children to support.

In economic terms France had fared very well inside the Common Market, with one of the highest growth rates of western Europe. But the distribution of wealth remained very unequal, with enormous discrepancies between rich and poor. Top French executives were better paid than their counterparts in Britain and Germany, and income tax was both lower and easier to avoid. At the same time, consumer taxes (which hit the low-income groups hardest) were considerably heavier than any other Common Market country except Italy, and it is probably no accident that France and Italy both have large and influential Communist parties.

Politically, it was abundantly clear that General de Gaulle was only concerned with his diplomatic campaigns against the Americans, and with his lofty vocation of making France once more a state to be reckoned with on the international stage. Despite his set-backs at the Presidential election of December 1965, and at the general election of March 1967, his towering position on the French political scene made him virtually invulnerable to normal democratic influences, and no one could have any illusion that he was interested in the condition of ordinary Frenchmen. It was the ordinary Frenchman, however, who was paying for the French nuclear striking forces, it was his money that was being spent on the relentless accumulation of gold in the vaults of the Banque de France, rather than on imports, roads or social services, and by 1968 it was no longer evident that the General's diplomatic terrorism was bringing any tangible compensations in its train. He had succeeded in antagonizing most of his allies in Nato, and most of his partners in the European Community, he had upset many of his countrymen with his attacks on the Israelis after the 1967 Six-Day War, and he had rendered himself internationally ridiculous by his support for the independence movement in French Canada. But in practical terms he had not won any real advantages for France. He had only succeeded in making himself a major international nuisance. Gaullists who are loyal to his memory believe to this day that he performed a valuable service in restoring to France a political stability that she had not known for 150 years and a dignity that had been shattered by successive military defeats at the hands of Germany. Yet there can be little doubt that in his specific objectives de Gaulle failed; a noble failure, some may think, but a failure for all that. Dimly, perhaps, the nine million strikers may have sensed that their awe-inspiring ruler was never going to be able to lead them to glory, and that even in the long run his quixotic tilting at windmills would never bring them any comfort. And if there is one thing the French do have, it is *le sens du confort*.

But whatever de Gaulle's previous failings, they were nothing compared with his glaring inability to deal with the May Revolution. At the height of the disturbances, he left precisely as scheduled on an official visit to Roumania on 14 May, and did not return until 18 May. For a further six days he did nothing to deal with either the riots or the strike, apart from intensifying the brutality of the police counter-offensives. And when he did act, on Friday, 24 May, it was only to appear on television to offer his countrymen a referendum on a group of legislative reforms that had by now become quite irrelevant. It was not entirely surprising that the street fighting escalated after the broadcast in derision and defiance to a fresh peak of violence, with 1,500 wounded and 800 arrested.

By contrast his Prime Minister, Georges Pompidou, appeared to be rather more in touch with the real world, and he gained in stature enormously by his conduct during the events of May. On the Saturday morning after de Gaulle's absurd broadcast, he started wage talks with the leaders of the three major unions, and when the bargaining ended at dawn on the Monday morning, he had conceded pay increases averaging thirteen per cent, and ranging up to over fifty per cent for the worst-paid. The fact that the strike was not being staged in support of a wage increase, or that the workers in many of the factories initially turned down the agreement reached between their nominal leaders and the Prime Minister, was neither here nor there: it seemed to offer the only available means for the government and the unions to reassert their shattered authority. For the disarray in the French establishment was virtually complete. For days on end it appeared as though France had no effective government, and the opposition parties were so confused as to the best way of taking advantage of the situation that François Mitterrand and Pierre Mendès-France, two of the most prominent Socialist leaders, seemed on occasion to be offering to take part in coups d'état — provided someone else took the initiative.

But at the last moment General de Gaulle reimposed his authority. On 29 May he flew secretly to Baden-Baden, the headquarters of the French troops in Germany, and two days later the tanks started to roll towards Paris. That Friday night de Gaulle gave a fighting speech on television, which prompted an enormous demonstration in the Champs-Elysées by loyal Gaullists flaunting tricolour sashes and flags, and it was clear that the General was winning. On Monday morning the strikers started going back to work, and in the general elections held (at Georges Pompidou's insistence) on 23 and 30 June, the bourgeois backlash against the rioters and the strikers brought the Gaullist party a massive landslide.

If the students of Nanterre had painstakingly planned an attack on de Gaulle's free-wheeling diplomacy, they could never have achieved anything as effective as the spontaneous reaction of the May Revolution. The immediate result of the flare-up was that a vast number of Frenchmen, both big businessmen and private individuals, reacted exactly as they had during France's many previous upheavals, by taking their money out of the country and changing it into foreign currency or gold across the frontier. At first this was perfectly legal, but they continued doing it secretly even after the government woke up and imposed exchange controls on 30 May. Inevitably, when all these francs were sold precipitately on the foreign exchange markets, the price fell, and the Bank of France had to buy them back in exchange for foreign currency (or gold, which comes to the same thing) in order to keep the rate at the level registered with the International Monetary Fund. In June alone over $1,000 million worth of reserves were drained out of the Bank of France, and, though the return to work and the Gaullist election victory helped to slow down the flood, they did not by any means stop it. In June the French government borrowed $885 million from the I.M.F., and in July it negotiated a $1,300 million credit with a group of foreign central banks. Thus instead of being a fully autonomous agent on the international scene, General de Gaulle was now, for the first time in ten years, to some extent dependent on the good will of his European partners — and of the Americans.

By and large his European partners were pretty sympathetic to the General's sudden economic difficulties. It was clear that the abrupt increase in wages and the massive loss of industrial production would seriously affect France's ability to compete, and most people (and virtually all Frenchmen) assumed as a matter of course that the franc would have to be devalued. What they did not fully appreciate was that the General considered the exchange rate to be an object of national prestige, and that facile and frequent devaluations were, in his eyes, symptomatic of all the weaknesses of the Third and Fourth Republics. Instead, he imposed import quotas for cars, household appliances and textiles, and introduced subsidies for exports. Naturally, such steps were illegal inside the Community, and Brussels hummed and hawed for several days in search of ways either of justifying them or else of preventing them. By 23 July the Commission felt that its honour was satisfied, and gave its blessing to the French measures for a six-month period, on condition that there was some increase in the size of the textile and appliance quotas. The Americans were less tolerant. They had their own balance of payments problems to worry about, and they imposed extra import taxes on French goods in order to nullify the effect of the French export subsidies.

At the time, there was room for considerable doubt whether the French measures would contain the effects of the wage increase. But before this doubt could be resolved either way, General de Gaulle received a further blow, with the Soviet invasion of Czechoslovakia on 20 August. If the Russians were capable of engaging in military adventures of this kind, then the North Atlantic Treaty Organization which de Gaulle had done so much to undermine suddenly took on an enhanced value. On 25 August Chancellor Kurt Kiesinger called for a high-level meeting to breathe new life into Nato, the German and American governments pressed for a bigger effort by the European members of the organization, and the U.S. Secretary of State, Dean Rusk, summoned a special meeting of the foreign ministers of Nato in New York on 7 October, to coincide with the annual meeting of the United Nations General Assembly. This agitation may not have led to anything very concrete, but it certainly discredited the Gaullist view of the Atlantic Alliance, especially after Manlio Brosio, the Secretary General of Nato, and Denis Healey, the British Defence Minister, had started campaigning behind the scenes in the autumn for the establishment of closer defence cooperation between the European members of Nato.

Despite all these political set-backs, it looked in the early autumn of 1968 as though the French government might after all be able to ride out the economic backlash of the May Revolution somewhat more easily than originally expected. The outflow of foreign exchange had slowed down considerably in July and August, and de Gaulle decided to try to accelerate the economy out of its difficulties. If French industry could expand its production very rapidly, it should be able to absorb the extra wage costs, and thus avert the risk of a devaluation. That at least was the argument, and accordingly the exchange controls and domestic economic restrictions imposed in June were released.

Having taken a buoyant view of the economic outlook, it was not surprising that the French government also stuck to its tough line on the question of British membership of the Community. When de Gaulle visited Kiesinger in Bonn on 27 and 28 September he managed to secure the Chancellor's total submission over the British issue, by threatening to take France outside the Community if the Germans continued to be difficult. And when Pierre Harmel, the Belgian Foreign Minister, returned to the attack with a new and more elaborate version of the Benelux Plan on 21 October, covering defence and technological cooperation as well as foreign policy harmonization, he was very rudely rebuffed by the French, who refused even to consider it.

By this time, however, it was already quite clear that the French economic strategy was not succeeding, and it had to be abruptly reversed. The dash for growth was working well, in the sense that the increased wage-earnings had injected an enormous dose of buying power into the economy, and industry very quickly made good all the output which had been lost during the strike. But this had not been enough to restore confidence in the French franc, and the reserves of the Bank of France were again draining out of the country – this time into Germany. The world's money market operators were now convinced that the German mark was undervalued, since the record export surplus of $5,250 million earned by German industry in 1967 was almost certain to be broken in 1968 (as it turned out, the actual figure was $5,750 million), and anyone who had money or credit to . spare proceeded to buy Deutschmarks.

The French central bank was not by any means the only one to be hit by the flood of funds in Frankfurt, but it was in a weak position to stand a second outflow of foreign exchange in six months, and accordingly the French government abandoned all its expansion plans in the middle of November, and reimposed exchange controls and a domestic credit squeeze. But even before they took this unavoidable step, they started changing their tune in Brussels. Right at the end of October, exactly a month after de Gaulle had cowed Kiesinger into submission over the British question, Michel Debré (now France's Foreign Minister) wrote to Willy Brandt to *propose* some form of limited preferential trading arrangement with Britain, and on 5 November in the Council of Ministers of the Six he not merely suggested that the arrangement might include a thirty per cent cut in tariffs over four years as well as some forms of technological cooperation with the U.K., but even agreed that the six permanent representatives in Brussels should study his proposal alongside the plans put forward by Belgium and Italy. (The Italian Plan had been put forward shortly after the Benelux Plan, and hardly differed from it; in fact it only existed as a separate document in order to satisfy the vanity of Amintore Fanfani, the Italian Foreign Minister.) In short, the French were so harassed on the economic front that they no longer felt able to reject out of hand any of their partners' proposals. Sicco Mansholt, the tough Dutchman in charge of farm policy at the Commission, who had maddened the French in July by saying that the Gaullist election victory would do nothing to help European unification, felt emboldened to call publicly on 15 November for a European summit to prepare for a new supranational Community. And Dean Rusk, the American Secretary of State, took the French shift of position seriously enough to say, at a meeting of Nato ministers on 14 November that the United States was opposed to any preferential tariff-cutting between Britain and The Six.

9 · The Deutschmark and the Soames Affair

By the beginning of November, the Deutschmark problem was assuming the proportions of an international crisis, for the flow of money into Frankfurt out of Paris, London and a host of other financial centres had swelled to a torrent. The whole world appeared to be scrambling feverishly for marks, and during the first three weeks of the month the German central Bank (the Bundesbank) sold nearly $2,500 million of marks for foreign exchange, and on 15 November alone it sold about $800 million. Time and again the Bonn government said categorically that the mark would not be revalued, but it made no impression. The business world was persuaded that the mark ought to be revalued, and the idea that the German government would long refuse to take the obviously sensible step was simply not taken seriously by the speculators. But if the market operators paid little attention to the denials of the German government, they pricked up their ears when General de Gaulle said, at a cabinet meeting on 13 November, that a devaluation of the franc would be the 'worst possible absurdity', and made sure that the remark would be leaked to the press. He intended to persuade the world that a devaluation was indeed ruled out; instead, he persuaded the world that a franc devaluation had been seriously considered, and that was enough to accelerate the flight of funds from France. He may not have realized that in May he had thrown away his reputation for immovable decision-making.

The following weekend, 17 November, the governors of the world's major central banks converged for one of their regular monthly meetings at the Bank for International Settlements in Basle, amidst widespread expectation that they would do something decisive about the currency crisis. It was reported at the time, and has not been denied, that there was something of a fight between the French and the Germans, with Jacques Brunet, governor of the Banque de France, asking for help in supporting the franc, and Karl Blessing of the Bundesbank offering support — on unacceptably stiff conditions. When the governors separated without making any announcement on the Monday morning, the flood of money into Frankfurt swelled once more, while an airy and unsubstantiated statement that afternoon by Maurice Couve de Murville, that all necessary support for the franc would be available, was universally interpreted as whistling in the dark.

The next day the German government, while still refusing to revalue, tacitly admitted the force of the argument for a revaluation by imposing a temporary four per cent tax on exports and a similar tax rebate on imports. This was tantamount to a revaluation of the mark on exports and imports, but since it left unchanged the price at which foreign exchange dealers could buy the currency itself, it did nothing to stop the rush for Deutschmarks. Understandably, foreign governments now started to get irritated with the Germans, and their irritation was all the greater because they had got used to the idea, ever since the war, that Bonn would always submit to its western allies. It was obvious that the mark was undervalued; it was obvious that the flood of foreign currency was not merely creating serious difficulties for Germany's partners but was even beginning to be an embarrassment to Germany itself: why on earth didn't they revalue and have done with it?

The Germans did have some valid domestic reasons for their stubbornness: German industry was heavily dependent on exports, and would not take kindly to any permanent aggravation of its exporting capacity. If it put up with the export tax, it was because it was, supposedly, a temporary device to persuade foreigners that there would be no permanent revaluation. Even more hostile were the German farmers, who accounted for about fifteen per cent of the German population. Under the rules of the Common Market, farm prices are fixed in terms of gold, though they are actually paid in national currency; if the Deutschmark were to be revalued in relation to the dollar and gold, then the price received by a German farmer for a ton of wheat would fall by a corresponding amount.

But the third, and perhaps decisive, reason was absurd. With general elections due to take place in September 1969, German politicians were already preparing for the campaign, and Franz-Josef Strauss, the demagogic leader of the Bavarian Christian Social Union, was getting a lot of mileage out of the Deutschmark issue. He posed as the defender of the national currency, and managed to persuade a large slice of popular opinion that a revaluation would lead to a rise in prices. The opposite would be true, of course, since imports would become cheaper and the slowing down of the export boom would also help to slow down inflation. But there were a lot of ordinary Germans who were naive enough to take his argument at its face value, and Strauss gained considerable populatity by posing as the sole defender of German monetary stability and the only bastion against the machiavellian tactics of foreign governments.

If the German trade-tax announcement only served to inflame the speculators, it also provoked a spate of angry messages from foreign governments, and Harold Wilson had the German Ambassador hauled out of bed for a late-night dressing-down. That Wednesday, 20 November, the finance ministers of the Group of Ten descended in an angry group on Bonn, in the hope of persuading the Germans to revalue. The French were by now almost desperate; the British were afraid that the French would be forced to devalue if the Germans didn't revalue, and thus undermine the sterling devaluation which was only twelve ineffective months old; and the Americans, though not under nearly such severe monetary pressure as the French and the British, knew that a French devaluation might turn the speculators against the dollar.

It was not a successful meeting. The combined pressure of the Second World War triumvirate and their friends failed to shift the Germans, and for the first time in over twenty years the German government asserted its sovereign right not to be pushed around by anyone else. Professor Karl Schiller, Germany's boyish-looking Economics Minister, asserted that his government could take no responsibility for the speculators, that the export surplus was a sign of Germany's economic health, with the implication that if other countries were vulnerable to the speculative pressures it was because their economies were sick.

His arguments were only sophistry, but in practice he didn't need arguments. If the German government decided that it would not revalue there was very little that the rest of the world could do about it. An inflow of foreign currency may be embarrassing, and it may even create substantial inflation by making domestic money too cheap; but it isn't crippling in the way that an outflow of currency is crippling. Conscious of the strength of their position, the Germans moved into the attack, by advocating a devaluation of the French franc, and they made sure that the proposal would reach the ears of the journalists gathered outside. This was undisguised psychological warfare, since it was bound to make holders of francs even more anxious to sell them. By the end of three days of fruitless argument, it looked as though the French government had after all no alternative but to devalue, since the German government could not be persuaded to revalue, and the finance ministers of the Group of Ten agreed to set up a $2,000 million credit in order to help France to carry it out. On Friday evening, at the end of the meeting, Franz-Josef Strauss, the German Finance Minister, triumphantly predicted to the press that the franc would be devalued, the next morning the French press confirmed his prediction by putting a figure on the amount of the devaluation – 11.11 per cent – and the German press carried banner headlines proclaiming 'We are number one.'

The episode represented yet another blow for General de Gaulle. Instead of resolving the international currency crisis, the meeting had only succeeded in turning the spotlights on to the franc. In fact, de Gaulle surprised the world that Saturday afternoon by holding a cabinet meeting in which he absolutely ruled out any change in the parity of the French currency, and instead announced a total reversal of economic policy in order to fight the currency outflow. This included a tightening up of exchange controls, subsidies for exporting industries, cuts in defence spending and in subsidies for the nationalized industries, a freeze on wages and prices, and an increase in consumer taxes. Lyndon Johnson immediately sent a message of congratulation and thanks. But there could be no disguising that the franc was still in the front line, or that if the Deutschmark stayed at its present level the franc would have to be devalued sooner or later. The strain on the franc was all the more severe because France and Germany were both members of the Common Market. Export subsidies and tight exchange controls were in the long run incompatible with the European customs union, and while the foreign exchange operators were somewhat taken aback by the General's decision, they were not persuaded that he could make it stick for very long, and continued to sell francs.

The economic consequences of the Bonn meeting were, however, less serious for de Gaulle than its political implications. For ten years he had had little difficulty in mesmerizing, blackmailing or cajoling successive German chancellors into accepting his leadership of Europe, and there can be little doubt that of all his diplomatic objectives the subordination of Germany to France was by far the most important. Now for the first time the Germans had thrown off the French yoke, and they showed every sign of relishing the discovery that they could stand up to the combined forces of the west. De Gaulle could take some small satisfaction from the fact that he had asserted his own independence, temporarily at least, by refusing to devalue the franc; but in rejecting the unpleasant medicine pressed upon him by Strauss, he had been forced to accept a total reversal of his economic policy, and in particular to slow down the development of the French nuclear strike force, which was one of the keystones of his diplomacy. De Gaulle could still surprise the world, and he could blame the troubles of the franc on the forces of 'odious speculation', but he could not conceal the fact that France's position was now seriously weakened.

Over the question of British membership of the Community France continued to take a hard line – and so did the British. At a ministerial meeting of Efta late in November, Fred Mulley, the junior minister at the Foreign Office who was dealing with the Common Market question, sneered at Debré's new trade offer and said that Britain was only interested in proposals directly linked to membership. But when the foreign ministers of the Six met during December, Debré insisted that there could be no question of a link between a preferential trading arrangement and eventual membership of the Community. On the other hand, he did agree that the new convention on patents being discussed in the Common Market need not, after all, be restricted to Six but could be opened to other European countries, and similarly that non-members could be invited to take part in the projects for technological cooperation being talked about by the E.E.C. members. By 17 December, Jean Rey, the President of the Commission, was sufficiently emboldened by these little tell-tale signs of a new French flexibility, to predict that by Easter the Six would be in a position to offer Britain a trade arrangement which would be the first step towards membership. In January, Debré was still opposing any link between the trade arrangement and membership, but at least he now tried to show that his trade offer was serious, by putting some more precise figures on the tariff cuts envisaged. Naturally, it was less than the Germans were proposing, and a great deal less than the British wanted, but it was at least a step in the right direction.

By the end of January, however, it was becoming clear that nothing could come of these preferential trading proposals. The French had dragged their feet for so long that no one put any faith in their intentions, even when they started stepping in the right direction. The Commission pointed out in a confidential paper that any preferential trade relationship between the Community and the British would be breaking international trade law unless it was explicitly designed as the first step towards the enlargement of the Community, and that, while the United States was still in favour of British membership, it would not stand for a partial tariff deal which would discriminate against American exports but would not lead to any strengthening of Europe's political unification. And in its annual report published on 17 February, the Commission noted 'a general deterioration of the atmosphere within the Community', and openly criticized the French government for its blocking tactics on the British membership issue.

For over a year now, the Benelux countries and Italy had soft-pedalled their plans for closer political cooperation with the four candidate countries, in order to give the Germans a chance to see whether they couldn't bring the French in on a trading arrangement, and so far the Germans had failed. By the beginning of February 1969 the Benelux countries started pushing their own plan again, with considerable support from the British.

At the beginning of February, George Brown, the former British Foreign Secretary and one of the most fervent advocates of British membership in an integrated Europe, made a lightning and unofficial tour of the Common Market capitals. The Foreign Office denied that he had been given any mandate to negotiate with the 'Friendly Five' on new tactics to circumvent the French veto. But when Michael Stewart, the Foreign Secretary, met his colleagues from the Six at a ministerial meeting of the Western European Union on 6 February, he rapidly reached agreement with the Five to embark on systematic mutual consultation on foreign policy – in short, to put the Benelux Plan into operation within the framework of W.E.U. The French merely 'took note' of the decision, as the diplomatic formula has it, and coldly announced that they would review the situation. The Germans managed to water down the plan, by insisting that mutual consultation must be entirely free and not focused on any pre-arranged subjects, and that defence and technology must be left out. But even in this attenuated form it was still recognizably the Benelux Plan, and Michael Stewart promptly proposed that all the interested members of W.E.U. should make a start by sending their ambassadors in London to a discussion of the Middle East situation. To anyone with a straightforward and sensible view of the world, all this must seem an intolerable palaver before what was, after all, only to be open-ended talks. But in view of the Byzantine arguments which had gone on between the European governments for the previous twelve months, it was not entirely surprising that Pietro Nenni, the Italian Foreign Minister, should have declared afterwards that the meeting marked the first step towards a real political Community in Europe.

When they had considered the situation, the French government decided that it was unbearable that Britain and the Five should discuss the Middle East situation, attempted to argue that it had a right to veto any subject put up for discussion in the Western European Union, and asked for the meeting to be cancelled. The meeting was nevertheless held in London on 14 February as scheduled, and though it failed to produce any startling new development in the attitudes of the Five and Britain towards the Middle East, the French announced on 19 February that they would boycott W.E.U. entirely from now on.

All very childish and petty, one might think. But behind the scenes very much more serious stuff was going on, which explained the apparently exaggerated agitation in the surface. On 4 February, only two days before the W.E.U. ministerial meeting, General de Gaulle had given an audience to Christopher Soames, the British Ambassador in Paris, in which he outlined his views on the future of Europe. According to Soames, who had his account of the conversation checked and approved afterwards by the French authorities, de Gaulle was apparently proposing a massive reorganization of the European scene. The European Community would be dissolved in a looser and wider European Free Trade Area, including Britain, the Six and other countries, without any of the supranational implications of the Rome Treaty. The North Atlantic Treaty Organization would be disbanded. And the new Europe would be ruled by an inner club of the four big countries – France, Britain, Germany and Italy. He suggested that there ought to be talks on monetary, economic, political and defence questions, and told Soames that if Britain were to ask for talks along these lines, France would responds.

There seems little reasonable doubt, in view of the care taken by Soames to check his minutes, that this was what de Gaulle said, or at least something very like it. In one sense it was not in the least surprising, since it corresponded exactly with all his known views on the Community, on Nato, and on the pre-eminence of the important states in Europe. Where doubt remains to this day, is over what he meant, or what he expected to achieve by rehearsing these views to Soames. If the ambassador had concluded that there was nothing new or significant in the conversation, the so-called Soames Affair might never have taken place. Instead, he took the view that de Gaulle was expecting an answer to his ideas. He may well have been right. De Gaulle must have been shaken by the discovery that he could no longer mesmerize either the French people or the German government, and he may have hoped, by an eleventh-hour reversal of tactics, to use the British to organize Europe on Gaullist lines.

The Foreign Office did not trust de Gaulle an inch, and assumed that, while the French approach *might* be perfectly serious, it might also be intended as a trap. If de Gaulle could lure the British into secret bilateral talks, apparently at British request, for the purpose of destroying the Community and Nato, he could at any moment turn the tables on them by revealing all to the Five. With hindsight, one need not assume that de Gaulle was *only* interested in laying a trap for Harold Wilson; he may genuinely have half hoped that he could, at the last moment, distract the British from their canoodling with the Five and make a final attempt to reshape Europe on Gaullist lines. But even on this interpretation, there is no doubt that de Gaulle would be anxious to ensure that he would be in a position to blackmail the British if things went wrong, and that for this reason, as well as for reasons of national and personal pride, it was essential that the British should take the initiative and accept the role of 'demandeur'.

After all these arguments had been anxiously revolved in Downing Street, Christopher Soames returned to the French with an extremely cautious reply. Yes, the British were very interested in what General de Gaulle had said, which they regarded as 'significant and far-reaching'. But they would have to consult their partners in the Western European Union, since their security and vital interests were involved (i.e., the British intended to consult the Five, since they would be affected both by the dissolution of the Community and by the break-up of Nato, but they did not say that they would have to consult the Americans or any other non-Community members of Nato. The U.S. was informed however, on 12 February, and Britain's Efta partners on 21 February, the day it emerged in the French press). They went on to say that they rejected the break-up of Nato, and reiterated the familiar British position that they were still seeking membership of the European Community. But on that basis they were perfectly willing to talk with the French provided the other members of the Western European Union were kept fully in the picture. In short, the British were perfectly ready to talk with de Gaulle, provided he understood that they were opposed to everything he had in mind.

This answer was conveyed to the French on 12 February, two days before the Middle East meeting of the W.E.U. ambassadors in London, and goes some way to explain why the French decided to boycott W.E.U. in future. A more important element in the French fury was the fact that Harold Wilson, who happened to be in Bonn on 11 and 12 February, informed Chancellor Kiesinger of the tenor of the French proposals a few hours before Soames had communicated the British reply to the French government. In his memoirs, Wilson has lamented that he was unwillingly manoeuvred by the Foreign Office, but other evidence suggests that he could not make up his own mind what to do and only raised the issue in his talks with Kiesinger at the last moment. It was quite fortuitous that he did so slightly before Soames was able to see the French in Paris.

For several days the story remained a closely guarded secret. But it was bound to break sooner or later, and break it did. Rumours began flying around Paris during a meeting of the W.E.U. parliamentary assembly, and the Soames affair leaked out in garbled versions in *France–Soir* and *Le Figaro* on 21 February. With what was perhaps precipitate haste, the Foreign Office immediately issued a full and circumstantial account of the whole affair.

Two days later Michel Debré accused the British on the French radio of 'diplomatic terrorism' – an ironic accusation to come from a Gaullist minister, in all conscience – and his ministry put out a very stiff rejoinder: 'French official sources deny, contrary to information presented with a sensational character, that the President of the Republic has, in the course of a recent talk with the United Kingdom Ambassador, expressed orientations different from those he has publicly and constantly defined in recent years. They indicate that today, as yesterday, France, which remains attached to the good functioning of the European Economic Community, notes that any enlargement of this by new admissions, and especially that of Britain, would lead to a complete change of the Community, and in practice to its disappearance. It would then be possible to replace the Community by a different system. It is recalled that Europe can only take shape on the political plane if the nations composing it agree on a European policy of independence.'

The next day, 24 February, the French Foreign Ministry handed Soames a formal note of protest against the British action in giving other governments and the press a 'distorted and unapproved account' of the affair, and stating categorically that there was no question now of going ahead with the proposed talks on the reshaping of Europe. But in the House of Commons that same day, Michael Stewart, the Foreign Secretary, said that Britain was still ready for discussions with the French (in the knowledge that there was no longer any chance of the French keeping their offer on the table), and pointed out, somewhat disingenuously, that the views outlined by the French President could not be both confidential and familiar.

On the detailed aspects of the Soames Affair, the French denied that there was any suggestion in what de Gaulle had said of a four-power directorate in Europe or of the dissolution of Nato, and on that same

100

hectic day of 24 February Michel Debré spent an hour expounding France's policy on Europe to the Paris ambassadors of the Five. But while an editorial in the Gaullist party organ *La Nation* said that 'mediation is not possible with those whose deceitfulness no longer has to be proven', an article in the same paper by Habib Delonde, the former state secretary at the French Foreign Ministry, appeared by implication to confirm that French policy fitted in with the British version of the Soames–de Gaulle conversation on all essential points, including the dissolution of Nato and the four-power directorate. Two days later, on 26 February, the French cabinet held its normal weekly meeting, and if the Soames Affair was discussed it was, for once, a well-kept secret.

Just what de Gaulle really hoped to achieve by his gambit of thinking out loud in front of Christopher Soames will never, in all probability, be settled. But the most illuminating comments on the affair came, not from London or Paris, but from the Benelux countries. The Dutch were entirely unsurprised that this was the way de Gaulle's mind was moving, since it was all of a piece with the way he had behaved for ten years. The Belgians, on the other hand, were touchingly disappointed that he hadn't thought of including them in Europe's new inner political directorate ...

If the Bonn finance ministers' meeting had marked a new low in international monetary relations, the Soames Affair injected into Franco-British relations a tone of apoplectic hostility. And when President Richard Nixon flew into London at the end of February on his way to address the Council of Nato, he only made matters worse by proclaiming the virtues of the 'special relationship' between Britain and the U.S. – though he repaired the error a few days later on a visit to Paris by agreeing to endorse de Gaulle's pet plan for a meeting of the Big Four on the Middle East, which flattered the General's sense of the importance of France and of himself as French President. The Germans screwed up their courage to flaunt de Gaulle and attend a second W.E.U. meeting, despite the continuing French boycott, but Kiesinger was obviously not looking forward to his next meeting with de Gaulle under the Franco-German Treaty of Friendship. When he got to Paris on 14 March, he was nonplussed to discover that the General, having been exposed in the Soames Affair, was determined to make the best of a bad job, and reiterated all his earlier arguments for reconstructing Europe from top to bottom. Completely baffled, Kiesinger changed the subject, and the two governments decided instead to embark on the building of a European airbus.

10·De Gaulle Goes

The Soames Affair was de Gaulle's last throw of the dice on the international checker-board, but he was still determined to make one last gamble in the hope of reasserting his position at home. Against the unanimous advice of his cabinet, he insisted on carrying out the referendum (on the down-grading of the Senate and the reform of local government) which he had first proposed at the height of the May Revolution the previous year. Not only that, but he determined to make this referendum a vote of confidence in his own authority, and he announced that if it were turned down he would resign. He had employed the technique of popular referenda on four previous occasions, each time to introduce changes of a magnitude which one might reasonably think needed popular support, especially if one shared the General's contempt for parliamentary government of the traditional French pattern. The first referendum was over the adoption of the constitution of the Fifth Republic, two more concerned the settlement of the colonial war in Algeria, and the fourth introduced the election of the President by universal suffrage in place of election by the French 'notables'.

This time, however, it was clear that the referendum was only a pretext for demanding a vote of confidence, and that the issue at stake was neither important nor urgent. As usual the General predicted the most frightful consequences if the French people were foolish enough to vote against him, but on this occasion his warnings made no impression, partly because for the first time in ten years it was abundantly clear that he had a natural successor as leader of the Gaullist Party – Georges Pompidou. Pompidou had been removed from the premiership after the general elections the year before, as a punishment for having been so very much more effective than his master in the May Revolution. But in the intervening six months he had not merely established himself as the Gaullist Party's favourite son, but had openly announced his intention of offering himself as a candidate for the presidency − should a vacancy occur. The referendum was duly held on 27 April, de Gaulle's motion was turned down, and de Gaulle himself immediately departed to Colombey-les-Deux-Eglises for his final, short-lived retirement.

It was perhaps a significant coincidence that, two days after his departure, the most extreme aspects of his nuclear policy started to be reversed. On 29 April, only eighteen months after General Ailleret had first enunciated the *'tous azimuths'* targeting policy, with the neutralist implication that French nuclear weapons would be potentially aimed as much at the United States as at the Soviet Union, the policy was reversed by his successor as chief of the general staff, General Michel Fourquet. Not only that, he also announced, in an article in the *Revue de la Défense Nationale,* that France would abandon its strategy of massive-retaliation-or-nothing, which had been adopted as a means of ensuring that any military conflict involving the Soviet Union in western Europe, however small, would immediately escalate into a major nuclear exchange and thus force the United States to join in on the European side. Instead, said General Fourquet, France would move over to a strategy of graduated response, whose object would be to delay the use of the biggest nuclear weapons so long as there was any possibility that the enemy would withdraw. This strategy had long been advocated by the Americans and the British, but they had only been able to introduce it formally into Nato after France had left the military side of the Organization. In the spring of 1969 it was no longer possible for France to operate a totally independent and unaligned military strategy, and with General de Gaulle out of the way it was no longer necessary to keep up the pretence that she could.

Georges Pompidou immediately stepped forward as the General's natural successor, but in the presidential campaign he was opposed by Alain Poher, a much-respected and modest socialist senator. And since Poher was unequivocally in favour of admitting Britain to the European Community, Pompidou found it expedient to take a flexible line on the issue. He had in any case to make sure of the support of Valéry Giscard d'Estaing's small Independent Republican party, which had traditionally lined up behind the Gaullists but was now showing distinct signs of wanting to live up to the 'independent' part of its title. On 2 May, Giscard send a warning shot across Pompidou's bows, by issuing a five-point communiqué on his party's policy which included the enlargement of the European Community to new members and the maintenance of the Atlantic Alliance, and Pompidou immediately accepted this policy platform. On 14 May, Pompidou followed this up by telling the press that he considered Britain's exclusion from the Community to be 'dramatic', adding hypocritically: 'Besides, General de Gaulle understood this well.' On 20 May Poher advocated, in a magazine interview, the immediate resumption of membership talks with the U.K., and on the same day in Orléans Pompidou said he would be ready to give the green light for negotiations – provided the British accepted the Treaty of Rome. With one eye on the Gaullist fanatics like Michel Debré, however, he added that Britain might be able to join 'some other entity' if the Common Market rules were unacceptable to them, an obvious reference to the proposals outlined by General de Gaulle during the Soames Affair.

At the next ministerial meeting of the Western European Union in The Hague on 5 June, Willy Brandt was sufficiently encouraged by these signs of French flexibility, and undeterred by France's continued boycotting of W.E.U., to propose that there should be a summit meeting between Britain and the Six in October or November, to discuss the enlargement of the Community. And the Christian Democrat Union, the senior party in the German coalition government, put forward an action programme on 20 June for the enlargement of the Community, the formation of a European Defence Council inside Nato, and the strengthening of Europe-wide democracy by plebiscites on major issues and a return to majority voting in the Council of Ministers of the Six in Brussels.

As usual, however, the Germans were taking too much for granted. By 11 June, the final run-off vote between Pompidou and Poher, it was clear that the question of British membership of the Community was not one which pulled very strongly at the heart-strings of the French electorate, and when Pompidou won with a majority of fifty-eight per cent, his hands were free once more to take a more ambivalent attitude towards the British.

In his first policy speech as Georges Pompidou's new Prime Minister, Jacques Chaban-Delmas told the National Assembly on 26 June that the Six would have to discuss the question of an enlargement of the Community very thoroughly before negotiations could begin – a striking echo of the blocking tactic adopted by the French Government in 1967. He also told the deputies that a devaluation of the franc would be 'dangerous and probably useless'.

The advocates of British entry nevertheless kept up the pressure. After a meeting of European socialist leaders, Willy Brandt felt confident enough to predict that a meeting between the Six and the four candidate countries (Britain, Ireland, Denmark and Norway) would take place before the end of the year. A group of 'Wise Men', appointed by Jean Monnet to report on the major problems raised by British entry into the Community, all duly added their weight to the judgement that Gaullist objections were totally unfounded. Professor Walter Hallstein, the former President of the European Commission, pointed out that the enlargement of the Community would require a strengthening and a streamlining of its institutions, with more power for the Parliament in Strasbourg and the Commission in Brussels and with a reversion to the normal majority voting rule in the Council of Ministers. Guido Carli, the Governor of the Italian central bank, announced that the reserve role of the pound need not create any obstacle to the admission of the U.K. and that if any difficulties arose for the pound they could easily be taken care of through the existing network of central bank arrangements in Basle. More impressive still because of his nationality was the report of Edgard Pisani, the former French Minister of Agriculture, in which he said that there must be changes in the Common Market's agricultural policy, to transform it from protectionism to open competitiveness, and that Britain's contribution to the costs of the policy under the present rules, amounting to about fifty per cent of the whole, would be 'manifestly unfair and impracticable'.

On 10 July, Georges Pompidou proposed that the Six should hold a summit meeting of heads of state or government, to discuss the completion, the deepening and 'if it took place' the enlargement of the Community. By completion, the French meant the completion of the agricultural policy and its financing rules. By deepening, they meant any other extension of the Community's common policies that might occur to them in the meanwhile. Only when the Six had irrevocably tied up the Common Market in ways that suited French interests would the French government be prepared to consider opening the Community to the British and other troublesome Trojan Horses.

Under the category of 'completion', by far the most important issue for the French was the financing of the farm policy, though they were still having difficulty in getting their partners to agree to common prices for beef, veal and dairy products, and had yet to force through common marketing rules for wine, tobacco and fish. Financing was the key issue, because the farm policy was proving increasingly expensive: inevitably the harmonization of farm prices had led to substantial increases of agricultural production, notably in some cereals and dairy products, because when a peasant finds the market price going down he tends to try to produce more in order to maintain his income, and when he finds the price going up he tends to produce more in order to earn more. And because Common Market farm prices were higher than those on the world market, the cereals and dairy products surpluses could only be disposed of with export subsidies, to make them competitive on the world market. And since the surpluses were mostly produced in France, as the Community's leading agricultural economy, it was essential for France that the costs of these export subsidies should be borne by the Community.

The interim arrangements negotiated in 1966 after the crisis would run out at the end of 1969, and it was now urgent to force the Five to agree to permanent rules; the question of British membership would serve admirably as a lever, as it had so often in the past, to maximize French interests. It was in any case vital for the French to ensure that the finance rules were wrapped up before the British could get inside the Community and acquire the right to take part in its decision-making. Britain was by far the world's biggest importer of food, and had the most to lose by the Common Market's farm policy and the underlying principles of its financing rules. As Edgard Pisani had pointed out in his report to the Monnet Group, the straight application of these rules in the U.K. would mean that Britain would be paying half the cost of the farm policy, and it was obvious that Britain would be anxious to alter these rules if she could.

The second French priority, that of 'deepening' the Community, was in fact a category without any precise content; all it meant was that Paris reserved the right to put forward additional demands which must be satisfied before negotiations could be opened with Britain. In the event, they picked on the notion of monetary union to fill this vacancy, and by the end of the year they managed to persuade the Five to accept it. It was a very curious choice, because the world was still being wracked by monetary upheavals and the European currencies were right in the eye of the storm. But then the French, while ever-ready to congratulate themselves on their logic and their cleverness, have not always been either sensible or consistent.

11 · Changing Parities

The speculative pressures on the Deutschmark had receded somewhat after the disastrous Bonn meeting in November 1968, but they gathered momentum again early in 1969, and by the spring foreign currencies were flooding into Frankfurt on a scale which dwarfed even the November rush. The stampede reached hectic proportions after 29 April, when Franz-Josef Strauss, the German Finance Minister, was reported as saying that the mark was undervalued, and that a revaluation of eight to ten per cent might be contemplated if a new international conference were to be called. No one knew why he had said it, for he was still publicly opposed to revaluation, but the effect of his statement was electric: on every one of the next ten trading days the Bundesbank was obliged to buy over $250 million worth of foreign currencies, rising to a peak of over $1,300 million on 9 May, and during those ten days the Bundesbank's foreign exchange reserves rose by $4,200 million.

If Strauss's allusion to a Deutschmark revaluation was an absent-minded lapse, some other members of the government were convinced that revaluation was now necessary, and the Grand Coalition was deeply split over the issue on party lines. Professor Karl Schiller, the Social Democrat Economics Minister, had competed with his Christian Democrat colleague at the Finance Ministry for popularity during the November crisis, by opposing revaluation. But by the beginning of 1969 he had come round to the Bundesbank view that revaluation was the only move which could effectively stave off the inflow, reduce the export boom, and thus cool down the economy and slow down the rise in prices. To begin with Schiller could get no more out of the coalition than an agreement that a revaluation might be negotiated as part of a multilateral realignment of exchange rates, presumably with France devaluing the franc; and the government justified its stand-pat position, by pointing to the continued French refusal to devalue. After an inconclusive cabinet debate on 5 May, the official spokesman, Conrad

Ahlers, announced that a resolution of the monetary crisis 'depends on a nation over whom we have no influences – we have no partner'. But the very next day he betrayed the government's uncomfortable awareness that it could not for ever hold the French government responsible for the undervaluation of the mark, by saying that a decision on the German exchange rate should be taken soon, adding: 'it could fall either for or against revaluation.'

Three days later, on 9 May, as foreign exchange poured into Frankfurt, the German cabinet held another session to thrash out a decision. This time Schiller proposed a seven per cent revaluation, but after a four-hour debate the Strauss faction carried the day, and Ahlers told the press that the decision was 'final, unequivocal and for all eternity'. But if the cabinet hoped that it would carry conviction in the world's foreign exchange markets merely by using strong words, it was living in a dream. Naturally, the speculators interpreted Ahlers' hyperbole to mean simply that the decision would probably remain valid until the general elections on 28 September, but that what would happen after that was very much an open question.

The coalition split was confirmed when Schiller clashed with Strauss in a Bundestag debate on the economic situation on 13 May, and on 14 July he publicly endorsed the report of an independent economic committee calling for revaluation But the prospect of a German revaluation after the September general election was too far off to bring any comfort to France, which was losing reserves at an alarming rate, and on 16 July, only five weeks after his election to the presidency, Georges Pompidou decided in secret to devalue the French franc. His decision was shared only with a tiny handful of ministers and top civil servants, and was not divulged to the majority of the cabinet until all the preparations had been completed three weeks later.

It was certainly not shared with France's partners in the Common Market. Yet in Brussels the next day, 17 July, at a meeting of the Six finance ministers, Giscard d'Estaing agreed to a new rule whereby each of the member states would in future consult its partners before taking any decisions which would affect the economies of the Common Market. He also persuaded the Five to agree to a plan put forward by Raymond Barre, the French member of the Commission in charge of economics, under which the Six would set up a reciprocal credit network for helping each other in the event of balance of payments difficulties. The details of this Barre Plan were gradually worked out by the central bankers of the Six, and when they were finalized a year later they included a $2,000 million network of credits for short-term lending, and another network of $2,000 for medium-term lending.

From the Barre Plan to the notion of monetary union was a short step, and it was not surprising that this was the notion which the French eventually chose to place in the 'deepening' category on the agenda of the proposed Summit conference of the Six. It was also characteristic of the French that they should decide to carry out their devaluation decision in a thoroughly Gaullist manner. Under the long-standing rules of the International Monetary Fund they were obliged to consult the Fund before changing their parity, and they had just endorsed a strengthening of the normal consultation rules of the European Community. They nevertheless took care not to consult either body. They had reason to know, from the success of their own spoiling tactics over the sterling devaluation talks in Paris during November 1967, just how damaging consultations could be, and they had no intention of being caught in the same way.

They also claimed that consultations had in fact taken place, at the Bonn meeting of finance ministers the previous November, when it had been accepted that the French franc might be devalued by 11.11 per cent. Since this was precisely the amount of the devaluation decided in July 1969 and announced three weeks later, they saw no reason to hold fresh consultations. Just in case this seemed a specious argument, they pretended that the devaluation decision announced on 8 August had only been taken 'in principle', and that before it was put into practice immediate consultations would be held in Washington and Brussels. All nonsense, of course, since it was inconceivable that a devaluation decision could ever be changed after it had once been announced.

The French devaluation immediately raised serious problems for the Community's farm policy. Under the rules adopted in 1964, the Six had gradually unified the prices of their farm products by fixing them in terms of the fictitious 'unit of account', equivalent to an American dollar's worth of gold. At that time, the dollar value of gold appeared to be the nearest thing around to an absolute and unchanging standard of value, and they thought that the 'unit of account' would confer an absolute stability on the equivalence of farm prices from Schleswig-Holstein to Sicily. A devaluation of the franc would therefore lead to an increase in the franc prices paid to French farmers, and while French farmers would be delighted by such an outcome, the French government was bound to be worried by the prospect of an upsurge in price and a sudden injection of extra spending power into the economy at a time when its first preoccupation was to slow down inflation.

An increase in farm prices would also be disastrous for the

Community, since it would inevitably encourage higher agricultural production in France, and add to the already mountainous unsold stocks of butter and other foods. So when the French held their scheduled 'consultations' in Brussels on 12 August, the Six invented a new rule, which said that France should have two years to raise its farm prices to the level fixed in 'units of account'. In the meantime, French farm prices would be lower than those of their competitors in the Five, and, since this was unfair, the gap must be filled by taxes on farm exports to the Five and rebates on imports from the Five. The episode underlined the absurd naïveté of having tried to fix uniform farm prices before the Six had even started to unify the rest of their economies, and the foolishness of the belief that any of them would in the last resort be deterred from taking sensible decisions on their exchange rates by the rules of the common agricultural policy. After the meeting, Gunther Harkort, German State Secretary for Foreign Affairs, echoed what many people were thinking, when he said that the decision marked the burial of uniform prices under the farm policy.

If Harkort was premature in pronouncing a funeral oration over the farm policy and its system of common prices – as the German government was to discover two months later when it finally came round to revaluing the mark – his comment was in tune with a growing body of opinion inside the Community, which was becoming disenchanted with the short-comings of the common agricultural policy. At the end of 1968 Dr Sicco Mansholt, the Brussels architect of the policy, had come to the conclusion that it was not achieving, and could not achieve, its original aims. In particular, he told the Six, the price mechanism by itself could not solve the social problems of the Community's enormous number of small and inefficient peasant farmers without imposing unacceptable burdens on consumers and national budgets. Prices were already so high that they were producing unwanted surpluses, yet they were not high enough to prevent a continuous decline in the real incomes of farmers. He therefore proposed a programme of structural reform, designed to make the farming industry more efficient and more competitive, which would reduce the farming population from ten million to five million by 1980.

At that time the Six were not ready to accept the view that their farm policy was a misbegotten creature, and the Mansholt Plan went into the pending file. But by the middle of 1969 similar arguments were coming in from equally authoritative sources elsewhere, especially in France itself. In June a special committee of independent experts set up by the French government to consider the whole farm policy reported that the Mansholt Plan did not go nearly far enough: the Brussels Commission had˙seriously underestimated the risks of agricultural over-production in Europe, and its proposal to take seven per cent of the Community's farm land out of production was 'derisory'. The Vedel Report (after its chairman Georges Vedel) went on to recommend that there should be a sharp cut in farm prices or, if that were politically impracticable, high prices for strictly limited production quantities, and that a third of French farm land should be taken out of production by 1985.

The Vedel Report created a sensation in the French farming community when it was published, and the French government was extremely careful not to suggest that it accepted any of the recommendations. But when Edgard Pisani published an expanded and revised version of his report to the Monnet Group on the agricultural implications of British membership, he inserted a recommendation that the Community should go over to a two-tier price system, under which farmers would receive high prices for fixed quantities, and lower prices if they exceeded these quantities. This was in fact the system which had been operated in France for cereals before the Community's farm policy was introduced. More cautiously, but moving in the same direction, Jacques Chaban-Delmas, the Prime Minister, told the National Assembly that farming must become a quasi-industrialized sector, in which the inefficient would be protected by subsidies, not by high prices, while Georges Pompidou put forward the argument at a press conference on 22 September that it was urgent to strengthen industry by drawing labour off the land.

More important, in some ways, was the belated discovery that the common farm prices did not always prove to be very common in practice, whatever the theory said, and were almost bound to be uncommon at a time of international monetary disturbance. On the foreign exchange markets, the most straightforward transaction is an immediate (known in the trade as 'spot') sale of one currency for another. But because the commercial world can often foresee well in advance when it will need certain quantities of foreign exchange – to pay, let us say, for goods bought from abroad – the foreign exchange dealers also provide a 'forward' market, in which it is possible to buy or sell currencies for delivery at a specified future date, which could be in one month's time, three months' time, six months' time and so on. One of the important differences between these two parts of the foreign exchange market is that each central bank is obliged under the rules of the International Monetary Fund to stabilize its own currency at the level registered with the Fund in the 'spot' market, but is not obliged to intervene at all in the 'forward' market. So the 'forward' rates for an individual currency can be very much weaker or stronger than the 'spot' rate, and in times of speculative movements of funds they usually are. During the spring and summer of 1969, the twin pressures of speculation against the French franc and in favour of the Deutschmark combined to push their forward markets very far apart indeed, and any German could buy three months' francs at a discount of at least ten per cent. So although farm prices were the same throughout the Community, German millers could effectively buy French wheat ten per cent more cheaply than German wheat, by buying French francs in the forward market. So much for common farm prices.

The approach of the German elections soon overshadowed these long-term anxieties, and created much more immediate problems for the farm policy. If the rising tide of foreign currency pouring into Germany was not as great as it had been in May, this was because a relatively small proportion of the May inflow had flowed out again, and the speculators were already waiting at the starting gate. No one expected the coalition government under Kurt Kiesinger to fall in with Schiller's revaluation arguments before the elections took place, even though the public opinion polls strongly suggested that the Social Democrats were quite likely to increase their showing in the ballot, and might therefore have a decisive voice in German monetary policy after 28 September. But Kiesinger did in fact take a large step towards the implicit devaluation of the Deutschmark during the final week of the campaign, by closing the German foreign exchange markets on 24 September. His immediate aim was to prevent any further inflow of foreign currency from expanding the money supply, thus undermining the Bundesbank's credit restrictions. But the practical result of his action was that in dealings in other financial centres like London and New York the Deutschmark floated freely away from the official parity of DM 4 to the dollar.

As predicted, the Social Democrats did make significant gains in the election, and though they failed to overtake the Christian Democrats as the biggest single party, they moved swiftly to conclude a coalition agreement with the small Free Democrat party. Thus a government led by Willy Brandt and Karl Schiller seemed to be assured, and with it a revaluation of the Deutschmark. In Germany, however, governments take a few weeks to form and to install, and in the meantime, while it was difficult to reopen the markets as though nothing had happened, it was psychologically impossible for Kiesinger to take a revaluation decision during his last days in office. Accordingly, on the day after the elections the German foreign exchange markets were reopened, and the Deutschmark was allowed to float there too. Ironically enough, at this very time all the world's finance ministers and central bank governors were holding their annual meeting of the International Monetary Fund in Washington — and the main subject they were discussing was whether or not it might conceivably be desirable to consider the possibility of introducing slightly more flexibility into the Fund rules governing the stability of exchange rates.

If the floating of the Deutschmark was received with resignation by the officials of the Fund, it provoked indignation at the Common Market Commission. The farm policy laid down rules for dealing with devaluations and revaluations which were quite clear, even if in practice they had just been proved to be inadequate; but it had no rules at all for dealing with a floating currency. There was no way of knowing what prices should be paid to German farmers, and to the tidy-minded officials in Brussels this was a scandalous aberration which must be stopped. In a fit of bureaucratic madness, the Commission tried to force the German government to peg the mark to a fixed exchange rate, by ordering it to halt all food imports — an instruction which, if followed, would have brought Germany to the verge of starvation within a relatively short time. Fortunately, common sense broke through, after a short and undignified legal squabble before the European Court of Justice, and as the mark floated gently upwards the German government was permitted to raise its border taxes to six per cent.

In fact, of course, the mark was not really floating freely in response to supply and demand. It was being kept on a very short rein by the Bundesbank, which nudged it slowly and consistently towards an undisclosed higher exchange rate. Everyone knew by now that it would be· revalued after the new Social Democrat-Free Democrat coalition had been installed in office, and the only question was, by how much? By gradually shifting its buying and selling rates, and by dropping broad hints, the Bundesbank kept the entire market mesmerized for over three weeks. And when the new exchange rate was finally announced on 24 October, everyone was surprised to discover that the revaluation was slightly larger than had been generally expected, with a 9.29 per cent shift in the parity from DM 4 to DM 3.66 to the dollar.

The re-pegging of the mark immediately resuscitated the question of common farm prices, at a special meeting of the Council of Ministers three days later in Brussels. But if the Germans thought they could reasonably expect the same tolerant response from their partners for their revaluation as the French had received for their devaluation, they were promptly disabused. The decision to allow France two years to realign her farm prices on those of the rest of the Community effectively meant that her market was partially insulated; if the Germans were allowed a similar grace-period, then virtually half of the Community would be cut off from the common price system, and the Common Market for farm products would cease to exist. It says a good deal for the new German government's 'Community spirit' that it accepted the validity of this argument, and agreed that there must be an immediate cut in the Deutschmark prices paid to German farmers. But in compensation it insisted that the farmers must receive subsidies to make up the difference in their incomes, which it calculated at DM 1,700 million (almost $465 million) each year. The Five admitted the reasonableness of this proposal, but initially refused to accept that the Community funds should be used for the purpose: if subsidies were to be paid, they must be paid by the German government.

Before the meeting was over, however, they relented enough to consider a small Community contribution, though it was not until early November that a formula was finally agreed: the German farmers would receive subsidies of $465 million a year for 3½ years, of which the Community would contribute $90 million in the first year, $60 million in the second, and $30 million in the third. And just in case this should be seen as a gesture of generosity towards the Germans, however small, it is perhaps worth pointing out that the sums involved were almost exactly what the Community expected to be able to save in export subsidies for French farm surpluses, as a result of the reduction in French prices. In other words, the short-comings of the farm policy were now being taken seriously not only by economists and agricultural experts but also by the finance ministers who saw what it was costing. The only thing that remained unchanged was the familiar pattern whereby the French got the ha'pence and the Germans got the kicks.

The financing of the farm policy was in any case starting to look like a serious stumbling block to British entry, not so much because of supposed British objections, as because the Six were themselves deeply divided, and it was perhaps no bad thing that the Summit meeting scheduled for November had to be postponed until the following month because Aldo Moro, the Italian Prime Minister, was unwell. Maurice Schumann, the French Foreign Minister, repeatedly made it clear that his government would dig its heels in over Britain unless it got a permanent settlement of the financing of the farm policy, and he apparently managed to persuade Walter Scheel, the German Foreign Minister, at a meeting in Paris on 9 November, that this was not just another French pretext for trying to keep Britain outside the Common Market. Indeed, he put such a plausible gloss on French policy that Scheel was able to tell the press after the meeting: 'M. Schumann and I agreed that the European agricultural policy must be altered to overcome the problem of surpluses. We also agreed that Britain must join the E.E.C. and that negotiations on the question must be started as soon as possible.'

All too soon – indeed, the very next day, at a meeting of the six foreign ministers in Brussels – it turned out that the Germans had once more misunderstood the French, for Schumann turned down flat the German suggestion that a financial settlement should be contingent on reforms to reduce the farm surpluses. But the French also faced resistance from other quarters in the Community. The Italians wanted to limit the new financing arrangement to another two-year period, for their food imports had shot up in line with their industrial prosperity, and they stood to be disproportionately heavy contributors to the farm fund if it were financed primarily from food import levies; with postponement of the permanent rules for another two years, there might be a chance that the Community would be enlarged, and that the balance of the voting strength would shift from the exporters to the importers.

In fact, it was already becoming clear that the farm policy would cost a good deal more than the levies could provide, and the Commission proposed once more that the balance should be made up, not by budgetary contributions based on a fixed percentage scale, but by gradually handing over to the Community the yield on industrial import duties as well. As in 1965, the Commission argued that it was unreasonable, in a customs union, that the Dutch government (for example) should keep the customs duties on goods passing through the port of Rotterdam, many of which would in fact be destined for Germany. The Germans, not surprisingly, accepted the Commission's logic, but the Dutch, the Belgians and the Italians all complained that it would be unfair.

November wore on without any noticeable progress being made, and it became obvious, even to the French, that they were not going to get a permanent arrangement for farm finance until the Summit had been held and they had given some tangible hostages to fortune over the question of British entry. They accordingly settled, at a meeting on 25 November, for a compromise under which the existing rules would

after all be prolonged for a further twelve months, on the understanding that a permanent arrangement would be negotiated in the
meantime and would come into effect on 1 January 1971. Even this
compromise was not achieved without a fight. The Italians and the
Belgians already felt they were contributing too much and getting too
little back from the fund, and they wouldn't fall in line until they got
assurances that the prolongation of the existing arrangements would
not be taken as a precedent for the future. The Dutch for their part
were very leery of the idea that the member states should hand over
their industrial customs duties as well as their farm import levies; as the
biggest traders in the Community in relation to their size, they
calculated that this would raise the Dutch contribution to fourteen per
cent of the Community budget, whereas Holland only accounted for
seven per cent of the Common Market's gross national product, and
they demanded that the transfer of customs duties should only take
place 'in the very long run'. The Italians, for their part, announced that
they would refuse to hand over their farm import levies if the Dutch
refused to hand over their industrial customs duties when the time
came. Even if they lifted their veto on British membership, the French
were obviously not going to win an easy victory over farm finance.

12 · The Hague summit

On the question of British entry, the weeks immediately preceding the Summit produced a number of straws in the wind which suggested that the French change of heart was sincere, even if they were still intent on exacting the maximum price for the opening of the door. Maurice Schumann, the French Foreign Minister, steadfastly refused to put any date on the opening of negotiations, and on 18 November forty of the more extreme members of the parliamentary Gaullist party formed a new group to fight British entry, under the title Movement for European Independence. But on 4 November Prince Jean de Broglie, the former state secretary at the French Foreign Ministry under de Gaulle, published an article arguing the opposite case. There could, he said, be no European technology without the contribution of British technology, no European capital market without the contribution of the City of London, and there could be no European reserve currency without sterling. 'It is on these three areas that the whole future of Europe is based,' he said, and he went on to suggest that the Six should compensate the U.K. for the heavy burden of the common agricultural policy by providing financing help for Britain's backward regions or for the international role of the pound — or even for the cost of building the Channel Tunnel. De Broglie was at that time president of the foreign affairs committee of the National Assembly, and two weeks later his committee issued a report strongly supporting British membership, on the grounds that it would offer political benefits for European democracy and would be in the interests of France, while another rejection by the Six would drive the U.K. into the arms of the Americans and would permanently weaken the Community. Meanwhile the French illustrated weekly *Paris Match* published the results of an opinion poll showing that fifty-two per cent of the French electorate was in favour of British entry, and that sixty-six per cent would be ready to vote for a non-Frenchman in a hypothetical election for a President of Europe. It was not of course in the tradition of Gaullism to pay any attention either to the electorate or to the National Assembly, but no one believed that Georges Pompidou would be entirely able to match his predecessor's absolute independence, and it was evident that he hoped to use the Summit as a platform for furthering French interests and his own reputation as a European statesman.

When the Summit opened in The Hague on 1 December, however, Pompidou was rather slow off the mark, and on the first day of the two-day meeting the proceedings were dominated by the new German Chancellor, Willy Brandt. The French President delivered only a short and ambiguous speech, in which he asked rhetorically whether the other members of the Community were ready to accept the French order of priorities — completion, deepening and only then enlargement — but painted no clear picture of the kind of Europe envisaged by the new French government. Brandt, on the other hand, was trenchant, categoric and insistent: 'The German parliament and the German public expect me not to return from this conference,' he said, 'without concrete arrangements on the Community's enlargement. By virtue of the Treaty it is one of the cardinal questions of our Community, and we must not put this matter off any longer.' He proposed that the foreign ministers of the Six should start working out arrangements for the gradual development of political cooperation inside the Community, 'on the assumption that it will be enlarged', and that a European Reserve Fund should be set up as a first step towards monetary and economic union. The working rules of the Council of Ministers should be streamlined, in order to make its decision-making procedures less cumbersome; the Commission's executive powers should be enlarged where necessary; and the role of the European Parliament in Strasbourg should be strengthened, especially in the control of the Community's budget. And if this programme of action did not provide enough food for thought, he told the French President that the German government would not agree to new Community finance rules, and would not recommend them for ratification in the Bundestag, unless it was sure that discussions of ways of eliminating the Common Market's farm surpluses would be started immediately and pursued energetically.

The forthrightness of the German statement apparently goaded the French into coming off the fence, for the next day Pompidou dominated the discussions by taking over and expanding several of Willy Brandt's proposals. He proposed, and the Five agreed, that new steps should be taken to strengthen monetary, technological and social cooperation in the Community, with the details of monetary

118

cooperation being worked out during 1970; and that the foreign ministers of the Six should set up new procedures for political cooperation by the following July, with a view to including the countries applying for membership. He also secured an agreement from the Five that a new financial regulation giving the Community its own sources of income would be drawn up by the end of the month, though in return he himself had to agree that the new regulation would include a strengthening of the powers of the European Parliament.

On the question of British entry, however, the Five got little more out of the French than imprecise and private expressions of good faith, and in the sixteen-paragraph communiqué it was only mentioned in paragraph 13, after a paragraph expressing the 'interest' of the Six in a long-standing project for the creation of a European University. It said that negotiations would be opened with Britain and the other candidate countries, but only after the Six had unanimously agreed on their negotiating position, and it set no deadline for reaching this agreed position. The only phrase that Pompidou would commit himself to, was 'as soon as possible and in the most constructive spirit', and the Five had to make do with an unofficial commitment from the French President that these preparations would be completed by the end of the following June. Afterwards the Dutch maintained that this private assurance constituted a firm deadline, but all Maurice Schumann would say was that: 'France sees no reason why the preparatory work, that is to say the definition of a common position, should take more than six months.' In short, it was still open to the French to drag out these internal negotiations for very much longer, if they felt they had anything to gain from delaying tactics.

In theory, of course, there was great difficulty in drawing up a joint negotiating position for the Community, since the Six had always agreed that Britain and the other candidates would have to accept the Treaties and the subsequent policy rules. If the British wanted any permanent exceptions to this principle, they would have to ask for them; but until they had asked for them, there was no way the Six could formulate a reply in advance. The bulk of the negotiations were bound to be concerned with the transitional arrangements — that is to say, the speed and the method by which the U.K. would move over from its own national rules and regulations to those of the Community; but it would be pointless for the Six to waste time discussing these transitional arrangements in detail until they knew precisely what the British wanted. They had a fair idea, of course, of what the British would be likely to ask for, since it was only two and a half years since

George Brown had presented his 'opening statement' at a meeting of the Western European Union; but it would have been absurd for the Six to have worked out a detailed negotiating position on the hypothesis that nothing had changed in the British approach in the meantime.

Nevertheless, there was room for argument over what ought to be included in the negotiations, over and above the content of the Community Treaties and their subsequent legislation, and the French tried to add a number of extraneous issues to the agenda, in a way that suggested they were looking for obstacles which might serve to keep Britain out. They wanted, for example, to hobble the negotiation with Britain by tying it to a satisfactory agreement with all the other countries in the European Free Trade Association, whether or not they were applying for full membership of the E.E.C. For several Efta members — Sweden, Switzerland, Austria and Finland because of their neutrality or their dependence on the Soviet Union, Portugal and Iceland because of the backward state of their economies — satisfactory agreements might be difficult. In 1961 the British government had tied its own hands by undertaking, in the so-called London Declaration, not to join the Community until all its Efta partners had reached an acceptable accommodation with the Six. Under the Wilson administration the Foreign Office showed no sign of wanting to make the same mistake again; if the French could insert a new variant of the London Declaration into the Community negotiating position, they would have a very flexible weapon for delaying, and perhaps even preventing, British membership.

In the second place, the French insisted that the role of sterling as an international reserve currency must be included in the negotiations, even though it was not a subject mentioned in the Rome Treaty. Here again, French intentions were highly suspect to the advocates of British membership. The French government could reasonably argue that Britain's long-standing record of balance of payments crises and its vulnerable position as a major debtor, both to the International Monetary Fund and the central banks, and to the members of the overseas sterling area, were bound to be of concern to Britain's future partners in the Community, especially if the Community did move along the road towards monetary and economic union as stipulated at the Hague Summit. What no one knew, was what the French would try to make of this legitimate Community concern: at one extreme they could demand, as they had in 1967 under General de Gaulle, that the reserve role of sterling must be totally abandoned before Britain could become a member of the Community — and that would effectively mean postponing British membership for an indefinite period, if not for ever; at the other extreme, they could simply be trying to reassure themselves that the British and the other members of the Community recognized the importance of the sterling problem as one that must be discussed and dealt with in due course.

In the event, the French abandoned the Efta problem, but they kept the sterling question on the agenda, and their partners and the British on tenterhooks, right until the summer of 1971. The list of negotiating problems drawn up by the Six three days after the Summit included agricultural finance, the transitional period, the Commonwealth, the institutions of the enlarged Community, the negotiating procedures to be employed, and, as it were in square brackets, 'economic and financial issues'; but not the question of the Efta countries who were debarred from seeking full membership.

The weeks following the Summit were full of hectic diplomatic activity. By 11 December, the five central bankers of the Community (Luxembourg having no central bank, since it was already part of an economic union with Belgium) came up with the broad lines of an agreement on a $2,000 million network of short-term credits which would be available to any member state in balance of payments difficulties, and it was adopted in a slightly more elaborate form by the Council of Ministers of the Six towards the end of January.

With unaccustomed speed, the Six also met the French year-end deadline for a new, permanent arrangement for Community finance. For 1970, instead of prolonging the 1969 rules (as they had previously decided) the Six reverted to a simple percentage key, under which the Germans would pay 31.7 per cent of the budget, the French 28 per cent, the Italians 21.5 per cent, the Dutch 10.35 per cent, the Belgians 8.25 per cent, and the Luxembourgers 0.2 per cent. But from 1971 to 1974 all the farm import levies would belong to the Community (less 10 per cent for administrative costs) and each year an increasing proportion of industrial customs duties would also be handed over. To soothe the fears of the Dutch and the Italians that the new rules would lead to sudden jumps in their contributions, it was agreed that the proportion of the budget provided by any member state must not rise by more than 1 per cent in any one year, or fall by more than 1½ per cent. Just in case the levies and duties were inadequate to cover the cost of the farm policy, they fixed yet another percentage key.

From 1975 onwards, all the levies and all the industrial customs duties would be handed over to the Community as of right (still less 10 per cent for administrative costs). If this were still not enough to cover the budget, the member states would make up the difference by handing over up to one per cent of the revenue of the value added turnover tax which would, by that time, be in operation in all the Common Market countries. For the first three years of this so-called 'normal period', there would still be limits on the amount by which the contribution of any one member state could rise or fall, but from 1 January 1978 this safety net would be removed. According to forecasts made by the Commission, the Community's budget might amount to something over $4,000 million in 1975; import levies might cover $800 million of this, and industrial customs duties a further $1,400 million, while 1 per cent of the yield of the turnover tax might bring in an additional $1,900 million, taking the total income to about $4,100 million.

The Dutch did not, therefore succeed in getting any permanent ceiling on their contribution, to keep it in line with their share of the Community's gross national product. But they did secure a small increase in the power of the European Parliament to influence, if not exactly control, the Community budget and the way it was spent; the French managed to ensure that it would be very small indeed, that it would only affect a very small proportion of the budget, and that it would only come into operation from 1975 onwards.

In addition to the progress made on British membership and the financing of the Common Market's farm policy, the Summit also gave new impetus to Community thinking about ways to combat the monetary upheavals which had been going on now for almost three years. It was clear that the farm policy could not long survive if its common price system and the exchange rates of the member states were continuously in jeopardy from the speculative pressures channelled through the international monetary markets. In a broader perspective it was also clear that the economies of the Six were becoming increasingly dependent on one another, because of the free movement of goods, money, investment and workers across their frontiers, and that sooner or later the member states would have to coordinate their economic and monetary policies. This was something that the French had always resisted, with the argument that it smacked of supranationalism, but since the May Revolution and the changes in the French and German exchange rates, the facts of life had become too obvious to be dismissed by ideological wishful thinking.

Yet though the French changed their tune in the wake of the Summit, they still clung to some of their old Gaullist illusions. They were happy to endorse the $2,000 million network of swaps between the Common Market central banks, because they believed that the franc was more likely to be in danger than the Deutschmark, and that the new arrangement would, in case of need, put part of the massive German foreign exchange reserves at the service of France. But they were still reluctant to envisage any permanent surrender of national sovereignty in the management of the French economy. On 24 February, when the six finance ministers met in Paris to put some flesh on the ideas for monetary cooperation thrown out at the Summit, Raymond Barre of the Brussels Commission put forward an elaborate eight-year programme for progressive coordination of monetary and economic policies, with the main emphasis on the monetary aspects. This was the point at which the French and the Germans took opposite sides, with the Germans for once taking a much more logical line than the French. Karl Schiller argued that the Six should go much further and much faster than Barre had proposed, with the objective of creating a complete monetary and economic union by 1980, in which all the major decisions on monetary and economic policy would be taken by the Community institutions rather than by the six national governments. The French, on the other hand, with the support of the Belgians and the Luxembourgers, wanted quick progress in monetary union, with the narrowing of exchange rate fluctuations between the Common Market currencies, but were reluctant to make any commitment on the coordination, let alone the centralizing, of economic policies. The German plan may have been excessively ambitious, even after making allowance for post-Summit euphoria. But it certainly made more sense to insist, as the Germans and the Dutch did, that any progress in monetary harmonization must be matched by parallel harmonization of economic policies.

Raymond Barre gradually shifted his weight behind the French in this argument, partly no doubt because he thought that the establishment of a monetary union throughout the Community would eventually force the Six to follow it up with complementary measures in the economic field. But it was foolish opportunism, and the repetition of a line of reasoning which had already been proved false. Many people had believed, in 1965–8, that the fixing of common farm prices in terms of gold would make changes in national exchange rates extremely difficult, if not actually impossible, and that the effective rigidity of exchange rates would therefore oblige the Six to coordinate their other monetary and economic policies. The error of this argument was resoundingly demonstrated in 1969, when both France and Germany moved their exchange rates but did not accept the consequences prescribed under the farm policy, and above all did nothing to coordinate their economic policies. The new Commission plan, for using monetary union as a lever for imposing economic union at a later stage on reluctant governments like France, was simply an attempt to put another cart before the same old stubborn horse. It was particularly foolish to imagine that it was a lever which could be used effectively against France, which habitually used more consistent and more rigorous exchange controls than any other Common Market country, and could be counted to do so again in future, if this were necessary to avoid the uncomfortable effects of a so-called monetary union. Nevertheless, as on other occasions, the French got a good deal of what they wanted, and by the time the six finance ministers parted, they had agreed to work towards fixed exchange rates between the Community currencies, and towards joint management of their gold and foreign exchange reserves – though they were a good deal less united about how they ought to go about it in practice.

Meanwhile, however, the Community in general and the French in particular were being faced with political incentives for making more progress in Brussels, under pressures which had their origins in the West and the East. On the one hand, the United States was taking a much tougher line towards Europe than it ever had in the past. The American balance of payments deficit was now beginning to cause embarrassment not merely in the rest of the world but also in Washington; but instead of acknowledging that the only effective way to cut down this deficit was to reduce the hair-raising costs of the war in Vietnam, the administration started demanding with growing insistence that the European countries should take over a larger share of the burden of Nato's defence of Europe. When President Nixon visited Europe in the spring of 1970, he warned that the U.S. could not and would not guarantee to keep its Nato forces at their present levels after June the following year, unless the European countries made a bigger contribution to the costs. Robert Schaetzel, the American Ambassador to the European Communities in Brussels and a long-standing supporter of European integration, delivered a parallel blast against the Community in a speech delivered in Bonn on 13 February. 'What does America think of the Common Market? Not much! In 1962 America was enthusiastic in anticipation of British entry; today a more uneasy America gives considerable attention to the economic and other costs, after Britain and other applicants are in.' Describing the Community as 'a tangled and complicated economic organization involved in inexplicable and endless internal argument', he went on to say that 'there is a strong feeling that Europe is insensitive to the economic problems and the political and military burdens of the U.S.'

At the opposite point of the compass, Germany's new Social Democrat government under Willy Brandt was beginning to carry out its promised policy to cultivate better relations with the Soviet Union and its East European neighbours, and was having a remarkable amount of success. On 8 December 1969, the Soviet Union agreed to open talks with Bonn, and on 13 February Egon Bahr left for Moscow as Willy Brandt's special envoy and had a meeting with Kosygin, the Soviet Prime Minister. On 22 March, Bonn and Moscow agreed on an exchange of consulates general, at Hamburg and Leningrad. Meanwhile, talks between the West German and East German governments started on 2 March, and on 23 April talks started between the West Germans and the Poles in Warsaw, and Willy Brandt wrote to Wladislaw Gomulka, the Polish First Secretary, to reassure him that the Bonn government had no intention of making trouble over the Oder-Neisse frontier between Germany and Poland.

No one could reasonably object to the new German government's Ostpolitik, and when he visited Paris on 30 January, Willy Brandt asked and secured from Pompidou the French government's official blessing. But it certainly wouldn't have appealed to General de Gaulle, whose main diplomatic objective was to keep the Germans in a position of passive subordination. When he spoke about German reunification – which he rarely did, and then with no enthusiasm – he argued that it was a question which ought to be settled by Germany's neighbours; in other words, it should not involve the Americans, the British nor the. Russians, and least of all the Germans themselves. General de Gaulle was no longer in power, of course, but he was still alive, and his loyalist supporters in France were constantly on the lookout for any departure from the policies he had laid down. But if the French felt uneasy at these signs of the German government's new-found political independence on the international stage there was little they could do about it.

Uneasiness was not confined to France or to Gaullists, however, though elsewhere the reasons were rather different. Few sensible people entertained real fears of German revanchism, but a great many 'good Europeans' had long considered that the unresolved problem of the division of Germany could one day develop into an explosive political issue, by accident if not by design, and that one of the main virtues of the European Community was that it would draw West Germany inexorably under the stabilizing influences of economic and political integration in western Europe. In the currency crises of 1968 and 1969, Bonn had for the first time stood up to its western allies in the defence of what it considered its national interest, and had shown every sign of having relished the experiment. No one could reasonably criticize the peaceful and sensible aims of the Ostpolitik, but many people wondered where it might lead, and wondered in particular whether its initial success would weaken Germany's support for the political aims of the European Community. In the improved Community atmosphere after the Summit, this was an added incentive for making more rapid progress in West European integration.

The third East—West incentive for pressing ahead with the Community came from the opening of direct talks between the United States and the Soviet Union, in the Strategic Arms Limitation Talks (Salt) which had started in Helsinki on 16 November 1969, only a few days before the Summit in The Hague. Taken together with the American warnings to their European partners in Nato, this dialogue between the two military super-powers pointed clearly to the possibility that the residue of the Cold War would be settled over the heads of the European countries, and that unless they resolved their internal differences pretty soon, they would be powerless to influence the outcome in any way.

It was partly for this reason that the Six agreed, at the Hague Summit, to make a new start in the political field, with the coordination and harmonization of their foreign policies; though it was partly also because the French wanted to fend off the danger that the Five and the British would finally put the Benelux Plan into operation, with or without them. In fact, the Five wanted the regular consultations on foreign policy to embrace not merely the Six but also the four applicant countries, especially the U.K. But they made do with a French concession to the effect that the four applicant countries would be kept fully informed of political discussions within the Six, and would be consulted during the course of their negotiations on membership, a compromise which was wrapped up on 6 March 1970. Most of the details were spelled out on 29 May, and on 5 June — surprise, surprise — the French ended their boycott of the Western European Union.

But then it turned out that the French wanted yet more concessions, to make sure that the countries outside the Common Market should not get even a nose inside the door until they had satisfied the examiners in the negotiations. Walter Scheel proposed, at a meeting of the six foreign ministers on 22 June, that the consultations should take place on two consecutive days. On the first day the Six would discuss foreign policy, and on the second day the same ground would be gone over again in an enlarged group including the four candidate countries. But Maurice Schumann couldn't take that, because, he said, it would make the larger group into a court of appeal from the discussions between the Six, and give the candidate countries a veto. So then Walter Scheel proposed that the Ten should meet on the first day, and the Six on the second day. Maurice Schumann still wasn't satisfied, because he didn't like the idea of the Six and the Ten meeting on consecutive days. The Five gave up the struggle against such absurdity, and acquiesced in a half-baked compromise, to the effect that a report on the discussions between the Six whould be conveyed to the four candidate countries. It was not as if the French had ever shown any interest in coordinating foreign policy with their Common Market partners, or as if there was any prospect that their debates would lead to immediate agreement on new foreign policies, or even as if there was any fundamental difference between the interests of France and the U.K. But the French government was still behaving, on the eve of negotiations with Britain, as though the U.K. was not merely outside the Common Market but virtually an enemy. The negotiations opened eight days later, in Luxembourg, on 30 June 1970.

13 · And then there were Ten . . . ?

Inside every long negotiation (to paraphrase Cyril Connolly), there is a short one trying to get out. The adversaries take up predictably extreme positions at opposite ends of the rope, and for months employ every device of obstinacy, brutalism and professional cunning to drag each other over the middle line. It is clear, right from the start, that each side will abandon the struggle rather than allow itself to be defeated, and that if there is to be an agreed verdict, it must be indistinguishable from a tie, as near the middle as makes no difference. The better the two teams know each other — and Britain and the Six had been practising together for ten years — the more clearly they can each see how the contest must turn out, even before it has begun.

Yet according to the rules of the game, no short cuts are allowed, every minute concession must be struggled for, each team must be seen to be straining manfully for the inconceivable victory — before the inevitable compromises are finally accepted. The forms have to be observed, professional skills polished in twenty years of international haggling have to be exercised, and, above all, each team's supporters have to be convinced that the outcome is the best that can be hoped for. Accordingly, the negotiations which opened on 30 June 1970, were squeezed for maximum drama and public activity for well over twelve months. *Je crois qu'ils aiment ça,* said President Pompidou with subacid mockery, after he had decided to put an end to the exhausting spectacle.

This is, of course, a somewhat cynical picture. Any reasonably informed civil servant from Britain or the Six could have forecast with great accuracy the terms that finally emerged, give or take half a per cent here, six months there, a tariff quota rather than a tariff reduction, one form of words rather than another. Together, seven civil servants could have concocted the essential terms within a week, if they or their governments had so wished. But what they could not have forecast with anything like the same confidence was that the negotiations would in the end succeed. Until the Summit meeting between Georges Pompidou and Edward Heath in Paris on 20–21 May 1971 a successful outcome seemed probable, but by no means certain. For the first ten months the French negotiators played a very tough game indeed, and while it never seemed plausible to suppose that Pompidou would have quite the nerve to pronounce a third French veto, it seemed perfectly conceivable that he might choose to drag out the negotiations until time or public opinion turned against the British government. Right until the very last minute his negotiators were making demands – for example, on the elimination of the reserve role of the pound – which were not merely a great deal harsher than those of their Common Market partners, but clearly echoed General de Gaulle's tactics of 1967. With hindsight it looks very much as though Pompidou had not made up his mind whether he wanted the negotiations to succeed or fail until his meeting with Heath: during those ten long months he had merely allowed the professionals from the Quai d'Orsay to conduct the negotiations as best they could, defending French interests and giving nothing away. There is little doubt that some of the professionals were only too glad to be able to make things difficult for the British, and must have been disappointed to see some of their best-fortified positions being given away over their heads without a struggle.

Thus, if there was any real drama in the negotiations, it was over the eventual choice between success or failure, and not over the terms. So it should be. The terms, by and large, were little more than a series of transitional arrangements governing the speed and the route by which Britain would adopt, and fit in with, the rules of the Community. There was never any question of introducing *from outside* any fundamental modifications to these rules, and neither Harold Wilson's government in 1967, nor Edward Heath's government in 1970–71, made any attempt to do so. The only important question was whether the Community should be enlarged; once that was settled, all the rest was merely *la' petite cuisine,* though in practice most of *la petite cuisine* had been sorted out before President Pompidou came to take his decision of principle.

Broadly speaking, the central framework of the 'terms' negotiated between Britain and the Six was a five-year transitional period, with some of the necessary changes taking place near the start of British entry on 1 January 1973, and others being held back until the end (or in certain special cases, after the end) of the period.

This transitional period is, indeed, a good example of the inevitability of the terms that finally emerged, since it had been obvious since the early 1960s that any agreement on a transitional period was bound to end up at or very close to five years. Why? Because one year would be obviously far too short for Britain to make the necessary adjustments, because ten years would involve unnecessary delays, because five is a nice round number in between, because there is no evident reason for choosing four or six instead, because the idea of a five-year transition has been in the air for a very long time. In practice, the five-year transition will be slightly compressed for the removal of industrial tariffs, and very slightly stretched for the adaptation of British agriculture to the Common Market system, but the framework of a five-year period remains untouched.

Within this framework four major problems stood out: the future of New Zealand dairy exports to the U.K., the future of sugar exports from the less developed members of the Commonwealth to the U.K., the British contribution to the Community budget, and the future of the reserve role of the pound. Together these four issues represented the key to the negotiations, because each of them was, in one way or another, vital to Britain. Butter and sugar were of great political significance, since both New Zealand and the Commonwealth sugar producers were heavily dependent on sales in the British market. The normal application of the Common Market's agricultural policy would effectively have excluded them from the enlarged Community market by the end of the transitional period, and the French tried to insist that the rules should apply to New Zealand butter and Commonwealth sugar just as rigorously as to Canadian wheat or Australian beef. But this would have meant economic ruin for a group of Caribbean countries who were already poor, and a serious set-back for New Zealand, and successive British governments made it a cardinal point of principle that no agreement could be concluded with the Community until a satisfactory solution had been reached for these two problems.

The British contribution to the Community budget was essentially a practical problem for the British — and a political/practical problem for the French. Britain is by far the world's largest importer of food, as well as one of the largest importers of industrial goods. According to the Community's definitive budget-financing system, all import levies on food and all import duties on industrial goods, plus a turnover tax of up to one per cent would be handed over to the Community. The full application of this system would make Britain far the biggest contributor to the Community budget, and would be a serious burden on the balance of payments. The British were therefore determined to make the transition to this system as slow and as easy as possible, by starting with a very low contribution in the early years of membership. The Six, on the other hand, had the strongest financial incentive in seeing Britain's contribution start as high as possible; the French argued that the starting contribution must be reasonably high, in order that the final jump should not be too steep, and they evidently suspected that the British government would find some pretext for not applying the full rules at the end of the transitional period.

The question of sterling was a symbolic problem. The French argued (with some justice) that it would be difficult to accommodate an international reserve currency like the pound inside the Community, not least because the Six were already committed to the establishment of a European monetary union. They therefore demanded that the reserve role of the pound should be phased out, and that the sterling balances (the reserves held in London by the central banks of the sterling area) should be run down. The British, knowing that any such project would take a long time to work out, and a very long time indeed to put into practice, and suspecting that the French were once more seeking a pretext for keeping the British out of the Community, did their best to keep the subject out of the negotiations altogether. In essence, the run-down of the sterling balances could only take place if the sterling area countries agreed, and if they were given some alternative form of reserve asset to replace their sterling holdings. Britain had nothing like enough gold or dollars to pay off the balances herself, and their run-down would therefore require other rich countries to contribute to some sort of long-term loan. Even if the Community were to participate in such a long-term loan – and the French government was careful never to suggest it – its arrangement would involve elaborate and prolonged international negotiations. The British government was perfectly prepared to *discuss* the sterling question, but it took the view that there was no pressing need to negotiate or settle it until the U.K. was inside the Community.

On these four central problems the two sides remained rigidly deadlocked in appropriately extreme positions for ten months. When agreement came, it coincided with yet another flood of speculative money into Frankfurt which dwarfed even the massive inflows that had taken place in 1968 and 1969. On Tuesday, 4 May 1971, the Bundesbank had to buy $1,000 million in order to keep the Deutschmark at its official parity of DM 3.66 to the dollar. The next day $1,000 million again flooded into Frankfurt – during the first forty minutes of trading in the foreign exchange market; and at that point the Bundesbank decided that it had had enough and closed the market. During the weekend, the Six held an emergency meeting of their Economics and Finance Ministers in Brussels, but after twenty hours of sometimes heated argument, especially between the French and the Germans, they separated without reaching agreement.

The Germans were determined to put a stop to the inflow, which was undermining all their attempts to slow down the inflationary boom by expanding the money supply in Germany at an alarming rate. But they were opposed on principle to the solution favoured by Giscard d'Estaing, the French Economics Minister, which was the imposition of exchange controls. They were therefore determined to adopt the only alternative strategy, which was simply to stop buying dollars offered on the Frankfurt foreign exchange market, and that meant letting the Deutschmark float freely until it found its own level. When the French expostulated that this would deal another blow to the system of common farm prices, the Germans suggested that all of the Six should let their currencies float en bloc against the dollar. This would, however, have had in some ways an even more serious impact on the common price system, since it would have meant abandoning, at least for a while, the farm policy's gold standard. The French might have been prepared to see a small revaluation of the Deutschmark to a new fixed rate, or a small devaluation of the dollar in terms of gold, but they did not want to relieve the American government of its responsibility for its enormous balance of payments deficit, by allowing the European currencies to float upwards.

The supreme irony of the situation was that, as part of their plan to move towards monetary union, the Six had decided to stabilize the exchange rates between their currencies, by narrowing the limits of fluctuation permitted in the foreign exchange markets – starting on 15 June 1971. With the breakdown of the talks in Brussels, it was clear that this particular part of their plan would have to be postponed. For on Sunday, 9 May 1971, the German government announced unilaterally that from now on the Deutschmark would be allowed to float freely on the Frankfurt market. The Dutch followed suit immediately, partly because they had had some speculative inflow, but partly because their economy was so very dependent on that of Germany. For similar reasons, the Swiss and Austrian governments revalued their currencies that same day, by 7 per cent and 5.05 per cent respectively.

When the German government decided to float the Deutschmark, it had no long-term objective in mind: it did not know how long it wanted the float to go on, nor at what rate the mark would be pegged, once it returned to a fixed parity, and it refused to give any commitment on either of these questions. The only thing it did know was that it was no longer prepared to take in dollars. As one senior civil servant put it to me in Bonn a few days later: 'Why should we be deterred from adopting a sensible economic policy, by the rules of a farm policy which no one believes in any more?' Sensible or not, it was further proof that the Germans were no longer over-awed by the French.

The next day in Brussels, at a ministerial round of Britain's negotiations with the Six, the French started easing back on the question of Commonwealth sugar. Instead of demanding that Britain's imports of sugar from the less developed Commonwealth countries should be reduced to half their present levels by the end of the five-year transitional period, they now proposed instead that the whole problem should be postponed until the expiry of the Commonwealth Sugar Agreement in 1974. More important still, they proposed that the sugar producers should be offered association with the Community. Though Geoffrey Rippon, the chief British negotiator, denounced this proposal as totally inadequate, it was clear that it represented a major concession. It was also clear from reports emanating from the Elysée Palace in Paris that President Pompidou had at last come off the fence, and had decided to play the negotiations for success rather than failure. After the French cabinet meeting on the Wednesday, the log-jam began to break up: that night, in a session lasting until dawn, agreement was reached on the method and speed of the alignment of British farm prices on Community levels, the French started giving ground on the British contribution to the Community budget, and Geoffrey Rippon accepted the French sugar proposal with the added rider that the Community would have as its 'firm purpose' to safeguard the interests of the Commonwealth producers when the Commonwealth Sugar Agreement ran out. The French remained immovable on New Zealand, but they agreed to insert another ministerial session to the negotiating calendar, on 7 June. Maurice Schumann, the French Foreign Minister, and Geoffrey Rippon were both able to agree that there had been a 'major breakthrough', and it began to look as though all the major issues could be settled by the end of June, the target deadline set by the British government.

Georges Pompidou may have been influenced in his decision to give the green light by the monetary confrontation with the Germans. But he was in any case due to be receiving Edward Heath for a two-day meeting at the end of the following week, on 20 and 21 May. By making a major concession on sugar, and by giving ground on Community finance, he could ensure that the Summit would open in a friendly atmosphere. For domestic political reasons, it was highly desirable that the Paris summit should also end successfully. But if it should turn out to be a failure – if fundamental disagreements emerged, for example, over the nature and the future of the Community – then Pompidou still had several key fortified positions to fall back on, including New Zealand butter, the future of sterling, and, to a lesser extent now, the British contribution to the Community budget.

In the event, the Summit was a great success. Meeting in great privacy in the Elysée, and for the most part accompanied only by their interpreters (Michael Palliser from the British Embassy, one of the Foreign Office's rising stars, and Prince Andronikov who had long served as de Gaulle's interpreter), the French President and the British Prime Minister quickly discovered that they were in broad agreement on many of the most important issues affecting the future of Europe. By the second day, they were able to move on from the exchange of generalities known in the diplomatic trade as a *tour d'horizon,* to detailed discussion of the concrete issues involved in the Brussels negotiations. By the end of their meeting it was clear that, while some of these issues were still unresolved, the negotiations were going to end in agreement.

Seated at a small gilded table in the same ballroom which had already witnessed two vetoes by General de Gaulle, Georges Pompidou told the world's press that Friday evening: 'The spirit of our conversations allows me to think that the negotiations will succeed'; and he added for good measure: 'It would now be unreasonable to suppose that agreement cannot be reached between Britain and the Community during the negotiations in June.' As if to exorcize bitter memories of two rebuffs, he said: 'Many people have thought that Britain was not European, that she did not wish to become European, that she only wanted to enter the Community in order to destroy it. Many people also thought that France was ready to use any pretext to impose another veto. Well, ladies and gentlemen, you see before you two men who are convinced of the contrary.' He had discovered that on some of the great problems of the world British and French views were similar or even identical, and while on other problems there were certain 'divergences', they did not represent the least obstacle to closer cooperation. 'The Prime Minister and I are conscious that this is an important moment in the history of our two nations and in the history of the European peoples.'

Just what they had said to each other on the 'great problems of the world' was not divulged. But the communiqué specifically pointed to two major issues which had not been settled: 'The President of the Republic and the British Prime Minister considered that it was desirable and possible to reach early agreement on the main outstanding issues in the negotiations for British entry, particularly the problems relating to New Zealand and the British contribution to the Community budget.' President Pompidou had remarked before the television cameras: 'Don't conclude that Mr Rippon and M. Schumann won't have difficult moments in the negotiations'; but he had added slyly: 'But they're used to that, and looking at it from Paris, I have the impression that they like it.'

Conspicuously absent from this reference to 'the main outstanding issues' was any mention of the reserve role of sterling, even though the two politicians were known to have discussed it at length, and it was widely assumed that they must have reached a broad measure of agreement on it. How complete this agreement was, was only revealed (even to the responsible French civil servants) some weeks later. What did emerge, through judicious leaks from both sides, was that Edward Heath had endorsed the French view (enshrined in the Luxembourg Agreement of January 1966) that majority voting in the Council of Ministers could not be used in cases where a government considered that its vital national interests were involved.

The excitement and euphoria (not to mention the sheer relief) spread across Europe by the triumphal success of the Heath–Pompidou Summit, was briefly overshadowed a few days later by signs of growing hostility from Washington towards the Europeans. At an international banking conference in Munich, John B. Connally, the Secretary of the U.S. Treasury, delivered a fiery speech in which he warned that America would not be prepared to go on carrying for ever what he called a 'disproportionate share of the common burdens in the defence of the free world', demanded that Europe and Japan should make a bigger contribution, and implicitly attacked the Germans for refusing to carry out their I.M.F. obligations to support the dollar in their foreign exchange markets. It was of course true that the Germans had contributed to the dollar inflow into Frankfurt, by their prolonged public debate on the merits of floating the Deutschmark, but Connally's speech was the sort of intemperate attack that one might expect from a man who knew that the chronic underlying American payments deficit had now reached intolerable proportions which could not be defended — and who was preparing the ground for protectionist measures to keep out imports from Europe and Japan. But what was even more interesting about the Munich incident, was that if the Germans had been uncompromising in Brussels with their Common Market partners over the floating of the Deutschmark, they remained equally defiant towards the Americans.

The Commonwealth sugar question had been settled between Britain and the Six during the first week in May — but it had not been settled with the Commonwealth sugar producers themselves, and it was clear by the end of May that the 'consultations' scheduled to take place on 2 and 3 June were going to require a great deal of diplomatic skill on the part of 'the British government. The governments of the Caribbean countries were looking with a very jaundiced eye on the Community's statement that it would be its 'firm purpose' to safeguard their interests in 1974, and they paid little attention to the Community's complementary offer of Association with the Common Market.

In Britain the political mud was being stirred by Lord Campbell, chief spokesman of the commercial sugar interests, who claimed that the Community's undertaking was entirely inadequate. But by the end of two days of heavy talking and hard lobbying at Lancaster House, most of the fourteen Commonwealth countries were persuaded that Association would confer really valuable advantages in trade and aid, and all of them endorsed an interpretation of the Brussels sugar agreement which was a good deal more specific than the vague form of words agreed by the Six. 'The British Government and other Commonwealth governments participating,' said the communiqué, 'regard the offer as a firm assurance of a secure and continuing market in the enlarged Community, on fair terms, for the quantities of sugar covered by the Commonwealth Sugar Agreement in respect of all its existing developing member countries .... In the course of the meeting Mr Rippon gave the assurance that it would be the firm policy of the British government to ensure that the proposals of the Community would be implemented in accordance with the statement recorded above, in the event of the U.K. joining the European Community.' Lord Campbell immediately welcomed these additional assurances as 'entirely bankable', and another dangerous corner in the Community obstacle course had been safely passed.

Three days later, on Monday, 7 June, the question of the reserve role of sterling was disposed of in Luxembourg with laughable ease and rapidity. Right up until the very last minute, the chief French negotiator on monetary questions was still insisting on a fixed time-table for the run-down of the sterling balances, with a ramrod rigidity which prompted his opposite number in the Commission to comment afterwards: 'He seemed to be carrying the sword of state in his throat.' That day Geoffrey Rippon read out a statement to the Six, which said that the British government was 'prepared to envisage an orderly and gradual rundown of the official sterling balances' after entry; would be ready 'to discuss after our entry what measures might be appropriate to achieve a progressive alignment of the external characteristics and practices in relation to sterling with those of other currencies in the Community in the context of progress towards economic and monetary union'; and expressed the hope that 'this statement will be regarded by the Community as disposing satisfactorily of the question of sterling and associated matters', even though it gave no precise commitment on the method or speed of the run-down in the sterling balances.

Though all of the Five knew by now that there was some Anglo-French deal on sterling, they expected the French to reject this statement as inadequate, and Raymond Barre of the Commission, who had prepared a detailed paper on the need to eliminate sterling's reserve role, clearly hoped that they would do so. But Maurice Schumann, who was in the chair, removed all uncertainties by immediately putting the question to Valéry Giscard d'Estaing. He accepted the statement as it stood, and sterling was no longer a problem.

If there remained any lingering doubts over sugar, they too were rapidly dissipated. Geoffrey Rippon circulated copies of the statement agreed with the fourteen Commonwealth countries the week before, and the Six raised no objection and made no comment. They had no need to, since they were not committed to accept the London interpretation of the sugar agreement; but it was nevertheless a relief that they kept their mouths shut. On New Zealand the French started giving ground, by proposing that her dairy exports should be permitted to enter the U.K. for seven rather than five years, while the Commission proposed that the British contribution to the Community budget should start at a figure somewhere between eight and nine per cent. Both questions remained unresolved at the end of the session, but when Schumann and Rippon gave their closing press conference they nodded in happy agreement at everything the other said, and it was clear that the end of the negotiations was only just round the next corner.

The two remaining big problems were neatly balanced for the final bargaining, with concessions required from France on New Zealand and from Britain on Community finance. When the ministers met again in Luxembourg, on 21 June, there was the usual preliminary struggle, with the French refusing to make a move on New Zealand until the British had moved on finance, and vice versa. The next day, however, the New Zealand problem was wrapped up, with an agreement that butter exports should be reduced to eighty per cent, and cheese exports to twenty per cent of their existing levels by the end of the five-year transitional period, and that future arrangements for New Zealand butter should be considered by the enlarged Community in the third year of British membership. On 23 June Community finance was settled, with the British contribution starting at 8.64 per cent of the budget in the first year, rising gradually to 18.92 per cent in the fifth year, and with limits on any additional increase for a further two years. Very rough estimates suggested that these percentage figures would give a net British contribution (after deduction of receipts from the budget) of about £100 million in the first year and about £195 million to £215 million in the fifth. As in every other case, these were the sort of terms which were bound to emerge in any agreement: the British starting position was for 3 per cent, while the French initial proposal was 21.5 per cent; the British had demanded a three-year additional period after the end of the five-year transition to limit the rate of increase, while the French had refused any such safeguard.

Apart from the last-minute problems raised by the Community's fisheries policy for the British and the Norwegian fishing industries, from a host of essentially minor nuts-and-bolts questions, and from the drafting of the membership Treaty, the British negotiations were now over. On 7 July the government published its White Paper *The United Kingdom and the European Communities,* setting out the terms and recommending without qualification that they should be accepted. The Great Debate could now begin.

If this Great Debate was conducted in essentially trivial terms, the responsibility was primarily that of the government. Although Edward Heath's desire to get Britain into the Community was never in any doubt, his administration hedged its commitment throughout the negotiations with the proviso that it would only recommend entry 'if the terms are right'. Until the White Paper was published, it refrained from any attempt to put across the long-term political and economic advantages of membership, apparently in the belief that a publicly proclaimed belief in the case for British membership would weaken its negotiating position in Brussels.

The reasoning behind this hang-back approach was absurdly confused, and only served to confuse the electorate. The 'terms' were not, and never could be, anything more than transitional terms, and certainly could not involve any fundamental alteration in the basic rules of the Community. If there was a case for joining the Community, on political, economic or any other grounds, it must be quite independent of these transitional terms, since membership means participating in an open-ended, decision-making Community whose future lies far beyond any conceivable transitional period. From the point of view of the man in the street, the terms could never be made to seem 'satisfactory', in the ordinary meaning of the word: it had always been known that the adoption of the common agricultural policy would involve a burden on the consumer, on the balance of payments and on the budget, and it had been known right from the beginning that the balance sheet was bound to be negative during the early years of membership. On the other hand, it was equally obvious that if this initial burden seemed likely to be unbearable, then no agreement would be reached in Brussels. There is absolutely no reason to suppose that the government's bargaining position would have been weakened by a more openly committed approach to the fundamental principle of membership; on the contrary, it is just possible that agreement would have been reached more easily in Brussels, and quite likely that British public opinion would have been less hostile to Common Market membership than it was by the time the White Paper was published.

So what is the case for joining the Community? Basically, there are only two arguments which bear examination. The political argument is that Europe is uniting whether we like it or not, and that the Community is already beginning to join the ranks of the super-powers. The Six are not yet politically united, but they already carry a far greater collective weight in international monetary, economic and trade negotiations than Britain does, and it is virtually certain that in time they will begin to move towards common policies on defence and foreign affairs as well. Britain is in every respect a European country – by its geography, by its size, by its history and culture, and by its economic structure; if it stays outside the Community, it will find itself increasingly dependent on decisions made by the Community, without any real power to influence these decisions. It is not so much a question of regaining a world role (though that may have its advantages too), as of making sure that future British governments are in a reasonable position to defend British interests.

The economic argument is much more complex, and therefore debatable. For the past fifteen years the Six have enjoyed a far higher rate of economic growth than the U.K., but there is little reason to suppose that the British economy could absorb the European growth rate by some mysterious process of osmosis. Some economists have tried to argue, absurdly, that the formation of the Community has had no measurable impact on the economies of the Six: the growth of their internal trade and the inflow of American investment conclusively proves the contrary. But how far the rapid economic growth of the Six is due to the formation of the Common Market, and how far it is due to other factors, is still not proven. It is difficult enough, at the best of times, to forecast the behaviour of the British economy three months ahead; how much more difficult it is bound to be to forecast, even approximately, the behaviour of the British economy six years ahead (at the end of the transitional period) after such a fundamental change in the ground rules as entry into the Community. The government and the Confederation of British Industry both believe that membership will bring long-term advantages in the shape of faster growth, but wisely the White Paper puts the argument in its most cautious form: 'In the light of the experience of the Six themselves, and *their conviction* [my italics] that the creation of the Community materially contributed to their growth, and of the essential similiarity of our economies, the Government are confident that membership of the enlarged Community will lead to much improved efficiency and productivity in British industry, with a higher rate of investment and a faster growth of real wages.' The assertions obviously cannot be proved or disproved until after the event; but it is evident that membership of the Community would subject British industry to much fiercer competition than it has known hitherto, and it is therefore probable that it would be obliged to become more competitive. The experience cannot be painless.

Yet in the last resort, most people have taken sides on the membership question on instinctive rather than (hopefully) rational grounds, measuring the Community against their chosen (or inherited) image of the present and the future. This is, it seems to me, perfectly appropriate. After the political and economic arguments have been exhausted, there is only one question which needs to be asked: is the Community now, or is the Community likely to become, the kind of organization one wants to belong to? It is evident that many of the protagonists on both sides of the Great Debate have been motivated primarily by emotional dislike of everything the Community represents, or by equally emotional excitement at the opportunities it seems to them to offer.

Obviously, someone who has an instinctive distrust of the Germans, or who takes sandwiches on trips to the continent for fear of being contaminated by foreign food, is not likely to have an open mind on the question of Community membership. Equally partisan will be those who see the Community as the only available salvation for Britain's declining economy. Yet it is curious that even the extremists have tended to concentrate their arguments almost exclusively on the 'terms', or on trivial individual questions, such as the government's right to give general directives to the coal and steel industries.

The trouble with the British is that they treat the Community more literally, and yet to some extent less seriously, than the Europeans do. There is a tendency on the continent to dress up Community affairs in terms of stern abstraction and to adopt a fatalistic approach to the negotiations and decisions of the Brussels institutions. This is partly because Community procedures and practices are strongly influenced by French practices going back to the ancien régime, partly because many Europeans are as impressed by pomp as by circumstance.

Yet even in the Community of the Six, reality kept on breaking through, and the formal absolutism of its decisions offers only a thin disguise for the pragmatic bartering of national interests. The conventions of Community discourse may be very different from those in Britain, but the political realities are remarkably similar. The stark logic of the farm policy can seem terrifying to anyone who is accustomed to muddling through; yet the exceptions and loop-holes which have already been introduced, for reasons of political interest or common sense, tell a different story.

Once the British realize that the differences between themselves and the continentals are more apparent than real they will no longer fall into a panic at the imaginary powers of the Commission or the supposed rigidity of Community policies. British civil servants already know how to take advantage of the differences of method: by temperament a Frenchman would always prefer to be chairman of the committee; an astute British diplomat would as soon be secretary, since the man who writes the minutes may in fact be in a better position to influence the final decision.

The terms negotiated in Brussels and Luxembourg cannot tell us whether we ought to join the Community, but they do tell us a good deal about how the Community works, about its essential role as a policy-making grouping with common institutions. As an outsider, the U.K. could not expect to change the Community's fundamental rules; as a member, it would participate in the making of rules, and there is no reason why the enlarged Community should not change rules which today appear to be immutable. This basic point is underlined by the type of solution hammered out for three of the four most important problems, New Zealand butter, Commonwealth sugar, and the sterling balances, each of which was referred forward to the Community institutions for a further decision at some future point in time, after British entry.

The solution to the fourth major problem, the British contribution to the Community budget, was in some ways even more significant: even though it did not include any specific review procedure, it underlined the general point that the institutions are permanently in a position to review past decisions, and will inevitably rectify serious mistakes. In a paper on Community finance prepared in the autumn of 1970 and approved by the Six, the Commission had produced a whole series of arguments (some of them specious) to show that the existing rules would not impose an unreasonable burden on the U.K. But it added an absolutely crucial precautionary phrase: 'If in the present Community, or in a ten-nation Community, unacceptable situations were to develop, the very nature of Community life would require the institutions to find equitable solutions.' The statement is so self-evident that it ought not to need saying: the Community exists for the sake of the well-being of all its members, not for the sake of the rules. Some rules may be uncomfortable for some members some of the time, but if the Community did not appear on balance to be conferring advantages on all the member states, or if the rules imposed intolerable burdens on any individual member state, the Community would not survive very long. That is why General de Gaulle's fight over the *idea* of majority voting was so childish and so irrelevant. No Common Market government has ever committed political suicide at home in its devotion to the rules of the Community, and none of them would expect a British government to do so: if the rules involved an unbearable cost to the British balance of payments, the rules would be changed. It is precisely as simple as that.

Naturally, the Community would not work very well if its members were always trying to change the rules, and would not work at all if they regularly insisted on changing them against the desires and interests of their partners. General de Gaulle employed the most brutal tactics in dealing with his Common Market partners, but it is far from clear that he really advanced French interests very much: the French are now facing the nationalism which the Germans picked up from the General. In short, membership of the Community only makes sense if one believes that it will be possible to reach agreement with the other members on mutually advantageous policies.

But is it reasonable to believe that the Community can in fact produce mutually advantageous policies? The record is not particularly edifying, and it has left a great many of the early idealists extremely disillusioned. To the casual observer of the past decade it must sometimes have seemed that when the Six were not having major crises, they were laboriously building a farm policy which was misconceived in theory and disastrous in practice – and which was diametrically opposed to every British interest. The reality is rather different. The crises and the farm policy marathons were indeed the dominating political themes in the Community's early history, and they certainly captured all the headlines, just because they were so dramatic. What did not get into the newspapers was the vast mass of minor accomplishments in the progressive liberalization of trade and payments, in the freedom of movement for workers as well as tourists, in the establishment of rules for fair competition as well as free trade – in short, the painstaking conversion of the Community from a mere customs union into a Common Market. Not all of the policies adopted have been ideal – far from it – and the process is anything but complete. But while it would be a mistake to ignore the marks imprinted on the Community by Gaullism and by recurrent political crises, it would be an even greater mistake to imagine that it consists of a customs union, a farm policy, and nothing more.

Perhaps the present situation is best described in the words of Bernard Clappier, one of the earliest converts to the European ideal, who was *chef de cabinet* to Robert Schuman in 1950 when the Coal and Steel Community was launched, and who is now Vice-Governor of the Bank of France. 'When I was much younger,' he told me in the summer of 1971, 'I was mad about the European Community. As the years passed, I became less mad about it, and today I am not at all mad about it. But if the Community is a great deal less dynamic today than it used to be, it is also a great deal more solidly built than many people imagine.' His attitude is symptomatic of the way Europe has developed over the past twenty years. Unalloyed idealism has given way to a more sober acceptance of the realities of international politics, and to a sense that, if youthful optimism has been disappointed, something valuable and enduring has nevertheless been achieved. The Community may not be a second Eden, but it does exist.

In time no doubt the logic of events will lead the Community farther along the road to federalism, but it will move along that road only as fast as all its member states are prepared to go. If Community membership today involves a loss of sovereignty, it is comparable to the loss of sovereignty involved in being a member of Nato, of Gatt or of the International Monetary Fund, and is considerably less than the loss of sovereignty involved in staying out and yet being dependent on decisions taken in Brussels, Washington, Tokyo, Moscow or Peking. Far too much of the Community's first decade was taken up with violent and futile struggles to dictate its long-term evolution. The struggles were inevitably inconclusive, and their only legacy was to make it more difficult to take sensible decisions on immediate problems. The future remains as open-ended as ever. Britain may be late in joining, but everything is still to play for.

Selected Bibliography

Action Committee for the United States of Europe, *Statements and Declarations 1955–67,* Chatham House–P.E.P., London, 1969

Albonetti, Achille, *Préhistoire des Etats – Unis de l'Europe,* Sirey, Paris, 1963

Camps, Miriam, *Britain and the European Community 1955–1963,* O.U.P., London, 1964

Camps, Miriam, *What kind of Europe?* O.U.P., London, 1965

Camps, Miriam, *European Unification in the Sixties,* McGraw-Hill, New York, 1966

De Gaulle, Charles, *Memoires de Guerre,* 3 vols., Plon, Paris, 1954–9

De la Gorce, Paul-Marie, *De Gaulle entre deux mondes,* Fayard, Paris, 1964

Deniau, J.F., *The Common Market,* Barrie and Rockliff, London, 1960

Hirsch, Fred, *Money International,* Allen Lane, London, 1967

Kitzinger, Uwe, *The Challenge of the Common Market,* Blackwell, Oxford, 1961

Lambert, John, *Britain in a Federal Europe,* Chatto and Windus, London, 1968

Lindberg, Leon N., *The Political Dynamics of European Economic Integration,* Stanford U.P., California, 1963

Massip, Roger, *De Gaulle et l'Europe,* Flammarion, Paris, 1963

Mayne, Richard, *The Community of Europe,* Gollancz, London, 1962

Mayne, Richard, *The Institutions of the European Community,* Chatham House–P.E.P., London, 1968

Mayne, Richard, *The Recovery of Europe,* Weidenfeld and Nicolson, London, 1970

Newhouse, John, *Collision in Brussels,* London, 1968

Newhouse, John, *De Gaulle and the Anglo-Saxons,* André Deutsch, London, 1970

Pinder, John and Pryce, Roy, *Europe after de Gaulle,* Penguin, London, 1969

Pryce, Roy, *The Political Future of the European Community*, Marshbank, London, 1962

Seale, Patrick and McConville, Maureen, *French Revolution 1968*, Penguin, London, 1968

Shanks, Michael and Lambert, John, *Britain and the new Europe*, Chatto and Windus, London, 1962

Strange, Susan, *The Sterling problem and the Six*, Chatham House—P.E.P., London, 1967

Strange, Susan, *Sterling and British Policy*, O.U.P., London, 1971

Tournoux, J-R., *Pétain and de Gaulle*, Heinemann, London, 1966

Tournoux, J-R., *La tragédie du General*, Plon, Paris, 1967

Uri, Pierre (ed.), *From Commonwealth to Common Market*, Penguin, London, 1968

Index